A DAVID & CHARLES BOOK
© F&W Media International, LTD 2011

David & Charles is an imprint of F&W Media
International, LTD
Brunel House, Forde Close, Newton Abbot,
TQ12 4PU, UK

F&W Media International, LTD is a subsidiary of
F+W Media, Inc.
4700 East Galbraith Road,
Cincinnati, OH 45236

First published in the UK in 2011

Text copyright © Cary McNeal 2011

The material in this book has been previously
published in *1,001 Facts That Will Scare The Shit
Out Of You*, published by Adams Media, 2010.

A catalogue record for this book is available from
the British Library.

ISBN-13: 978-1-4463-0041-1 paperback
ISBN-10: 1-4463-0041-2 paperback

Printed in China by RR Donnelley
for F&W Media International LTD,
Brunel House, Forde Close, Newton Abbot,
TQ12 4PU, UK

10 9 8 7 6 5 4 3 2 1

Senior Acquisitions Editor: Freya Dangerfield
Assistant Editor: Felicity Barr
Project Editor: Verity Muir
Senior Designer: Jodie Lystor
Senior Production Controller: Kelly Smith

David & Charles publish high quality books on a
wide range of subjects.
For more great book ideas visit:
www.rubooks.co.uk

Contents

INTRODUCTION

The World is a frightening place.

But you already knew that; you read it in the paper, hear about it from friends, see it with your own eyes every time you turn on the TV to watch bad singers or dancers subject themselves to abuse from judges with no more talent than the contestants, or see a web video of a teenager shooting a bottle rocket from his arse for amusement, or get plowed from behind in your car by another driver who was texting 'LMAO' to his friends.

If random violence doesn't get you, cancer will. If cancer doesn't, global warming will. If global warming doesn't, bullet ants will. Or botflies. Or lightning. Or tsunamis. Or just normal everyday activities like drinking water, eating an orange, breathing the air, or having sex with a goat.

Yes, we are in deep doo-doo. You should be scared to death, right? Wrong.

Okay, this is a book of scary facts, and the more you read, the more afraid you are likely to be. But if forewarned is forearmed, then the more you know, the safer you'll feel, even if it's a false sense of security since you can't do a thing about most of what you read here. But who cares, as long as you feel better?

If not – if this scares the shit out of you – that's okay, too. You're probably reading this on the crapper, anyway, and what better place to be scared shitless? Isn't that the idea, to be shitless?

At least you aren't befouling a nice pair of pants. I'm also keeping you regular. You're welcome.

While I'm scaring you, though, I also hope to make you laugh.

There's a joke after every fact, for goodness sakes. Do you have any idea how hard it is to make jokes about things like a guy getting the wrong testicle removed during surgery? Okay, bad example. But you get the idea: you should laugh when you read this book. If you don't, either you have no sense of humour or I need a new career. I'm too old to start a new career, so the blame falls squarely on you.

Be warned also that you might be offended by this book when I make fun of someone or something you love. Butts of my jokes include doctors, dentists, Latvians, Texans, children, pets, Deadheads, mothers-in-law, Death Row inmates, Catholics, Pentecostals, the French, Tennessee, fast-food employees, and numerous other people, places and things. I also make ample fun of myself, my wife, my (fictitious) sex life, and other things I hold near and dear. So unbunch your pants and laugh a little.

Far more offensive than my jokes are the ridiculous things that occur in this world on a daily basis, so read these facts and be afraid, be amused, be annoyed, be aghast, be whatever. You already bought the book and I already got paid, so I don't really care. Sorry, just being honest. (Sort of.)

And remember: front to back, and keep wiping until clean.

Your pal,

Cary McNeal

Acknowledgments

Writing any book is a massive undertaking, and no author does it alone, even though you certainly feel alone when it's 4:30 on a beautiful sunny spring afternoon and you're stuck inside banging your head against the desk as you try to come up with something funny to say about people being beheaded or bugs that eat human flesh while all your friends and family are outside somewhere having fun without you, usually accompanied by alcohol.

Still, a lot of people made this book happen, and I need to thank them. Especially if I want to get hired again. Those people are:

Holly Schmidt and Allan Penn at Hollan Publishing, for giving me the opportunity to write this book, for believing in me, for coddling me and listening to me whine and bitch about how hard it was and convincing me it would be worth the effort in the end. It was.

Matt Glazer and Paula Munier at Adams Media, for their guidance and patience, and for giving a first-time author a chance.

Kirsten Amman, my researcher, whose task was monumental; yet she did it with vigor and efficiency and glee. For that I could kiss her, but I don't want her boyfriend to beat my ass, so she'll have settle for a heartfelt thank you.

Jenny Bent of The Bent Agency, for her generous and invaluable advice, and Elaine English, my attorney, for reading all the long, wordy documents and knowing exactly which parts were most important.

My friends Don and Danna Calder, for legal assistance, medical supervision, patience, and encouragement, and for entertaining my family while I was holed up writing.

Beverly Linzer Jenkins and Adrianne Gershberg, the funniest chicks I know, for their comic genius and inspiration, and all my friends from List of the Day.

Amy Miller and Tom Jacobsen for their unconditional friendship and for waiting months for me to answer their e-mails and return their phone calls.

Amy Winter, my professional role model and friend, and the entire crew at Wolff Bros Post.

My parents, Perry and Jean McNeal, and the rest of my family for their interest in, and support of, my writing.

My wife Paige and daughter Keaton for loving me no matter what.

What the _?!

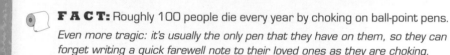

The worst and worst of the weirdest in the world

F A C T: Roughly 100 people die every year by choking on ball-point pens.

Even more tragic: it's usually the only pen that they have on them, so they can forget writing a quick farewell note to their loved ones as they are choking.

• Mitchell Symons, This Book:. . . of More Perfectly Useless Information (Harper Collins, 2005).

F A C T: Some scientists view love in terms of addiction, and they might be right. One study discovered that monogamous pairing is based in the same region of the brain as drug addiction. Losing your love can be like experiencing withdrawal.

And for some, getting divorced can feel like taking ecstasy.

• Susana Martinez-Conde and Stephen L. Macknik, "Optical Illusions and the Illusion of Love," Scientific American, February 12, 2009, www.sciam.com.

F A C T: Studies that examined what victims of a heart attack were doing and feeling in the hours preceding the event found acute emotional stress to be a common trigger. In one study, more than half of subjects reported being very upset or under great stress in the 24 hours before their attack.

But probably not as upset as they were during and after the attack.

• Michael Feld and Johann Caspar Ruegg, "Head Attack," Scientific American, June 2005, www.sciam.com

 F A C T: A 2000 survey on driving habits ranks tuning the radio as the most common distraction, with over 60 per cent of drivers admitting that they do it. Other distractions noted include eating while driving (57 per cent), and turning around to talk with passengers (56 per cent). Surprisingly, only a third of drivers listed talking on a mobile phone as a distraction.

Because the other two-thirds of mobile users aren't distracted at all. They give the phone call their full attention while barreling their car through anything in the way: stop signs, road works crews, OAPs, dogs, children, the blind, traffic wardens, cyclists, unicyclists, juggling unicyclists, mimes, midget parades, clown funerals, etc.

• "The 10 Most Dangerous Foods to Eat While Driving," Insurance.com, March 2, 2007, www.insurance.com.

 F A C T: Studies show that 87 per cent of people fear getting trapped in dull conversations at dinner parties.

If someone is boring you to tears, interrupt and ask if he would mind calling you on your mobile phone. Tell him you want to check reception. When he does, and your phone rings, answer it and say, 'Hello?' Then cover the mouthpiece and say to him, 'I need to take this, sorry'.

• Richard Wiseman, Quirkology: How We Discover the Big Truths in Small Things (Basic Books, 2008).

 F A C T: Women with cosmetic breast implants are three times more likely than other women to take their own lives, and are also three times as likely to die from alcohol and drug use. Why? Researchers suspect that many of these women had pre-existing body image and self-esteem issues before getting the implants.

Nah, the researchers – obviously female – are just jealous of women with fabulous racks.

• Maggie Fox, "Breast Implants Linked with Suicide in Study," Reuters, Aug 8, 2007, www.reuters.com.

F A C T: Teenager Natalie Cooper is unable to eat anything but Tic-Tacs, and throws up anything else she tries to ingest. Cooper must be fed a special formula through a tube to her stomach in order to survive.

She'd have great breath if it weren't for all the puking.

• "The teenage girl who can only eat Tic Tacs," The Daily Mail, February 9, 2008, www.dailymail.co.uk.

F A C T: In 2008, a fifty-year-old woman from Saudi Arabia demanded a divorce in 2008 after her husband lifted her veil to view her face while she was asleep. She had concealed her face from him for thirty years.

Because she looks like Mickey Rourke.

• "Divorce for Looking at Wife's Face," The Daily Telegraph, May 21, 2008, www.news.com.au.

F A C T: In January 2008, domestic violence expert Dean Tong was arrested for assaulting his wife. This was Tong's third arrest, and his second involving domestic violence.

How do you think he became an expert?

• Susan Wilson, "Update: Abuse Expert Arrested on Abuse Charge Releases Statement," Tampa Bay's 10 News, www.wtsp.com.
• Melanie Brooks, "Author Under Arrest Talks Exclusively with 10 News," 10Connects.com, www.wtsp.com.

F A C T: A retired teacher in California admits that he taught high school for seventeen years without knowing how to read or write.

Neither could his students, so it all worked out.

• Charisse Yu, "Retired Teacher Reveals He Was Illitreate Until Age 48," 10 News San Diego, February 14, 2008, www.10news.com.

F A C T: A man nearly died at an airport security checkpoint in Nuremberg in 2007 after drinking a full litre of vodka rather than surrendering it before taking his flight. The man became impaired and had to be taken to a hospital and treated for alcohol poisoning.

Unfortunately, he was one of the pilots, so the flight was delayed until someone else could be called in to take his place.

• Associated Press, "Man Chugs Down Litre of Vodka in Airport Line," USA Today, December 12, 2007, www.usatoday.com.

 F A C T: A New York man faced arrest in Times Square in 2004 for doing nothing. A police officer charged Matthew Jones with 'disorderly conduct' because 'numerous pedestrians in the area had to walk around him.' Jones maintains he was simply 'standing around' talking to friends.

If standing around doing nothing is a crime, I know a lot of people who should be in jail.

• Nicholas Confessore, "A Times Square Pedestrian Is Giving No Ground," New York Times, October 18, 2007, www.nytimes.com.

 F A C T: 40 per cent of women admit that they have thrown footwear at a man.

Women love shoes, so if she's willing to hurl one at you, you know she's pissed off.

• Bernice Kanner, Are You Normal about Sex, Love, and Relationships? (Macmillan, 2004).

 F A C T: A Nevada couple were charged in 2007 with child neglect after their kids became malnourished while the couple played online video games for days at a time. Their eleven-month-old's hair was so matted that her head had to be shaved, and her twenty-two-month-old brother had difficulty walking due to lack of muscle development.

Video games may or may not be addictive, but being an arse hole certainly is.

• Associated Press, "Parents Neglect Starved Babies to Feed Video Game Addiction," Fox News, July 14, 2007, www.foxnews.com.

 F A C T: In 2007 a British climber reached the summit of Mt. Everest, but ran out of air during his descent. As many as forty climbers passed the dying man, unwilling to risk using up their own oxygen to help him.

They'll need it in Hell.

• Associated Press, "As Others Pass, Climber Dies Alone on Mount Everest,"ESPN, May 27, 2006, http://sports.espn.go.com.

FACT: A former U.S. soldier who was wounded in Iraq was billed for his bloody body armour that was discarded as a biohazard. The man, who left the Army because of his injury, had to borrow $700 from friends to make the payment before the Army would discharge him.

Oh, and thanks for serving!

• Allison Barker for the Associated Press, "Wounded Soldier Made To Pay For Armor Pulled Off His Bleeding Body," The Huffington Post, February 8, 2006, www.huffingtonpost.com.

FACT: Multimillionaire David Pizer has arranged to freeze his body in liquid nitrogen when he dies in hope of being brought back to life one day. Pizer has also left his entire fortune to himself.

I hope he's not counting on his heirs to unfreeze him.

• James Langton, "Rich Freeze Their Assets for Chance to Live Again," Telegraph UK, January 30, 2006, www.telegraph.co.uk.

FACT: A French woman who survived the first face transplant in history in 2006 took up smoking again once she regained feeling in her mouth and lips.

She spent months in the hospital and had umpteen surgeries after having half of her face chewed off by her dog while she was passed out after attempting suicide with a handful of sleeping pills. Let the woman have a damn cigarette.

• Ariane Bernard and Craig S.Smith, "French Face-Transplant Patient Tells of Her Ordeal," New York Times, February 7, 2006, www.nytimes.com.

FACT: In 2006, a forty-one-year-old British woman married what she called 'the love of my life': a male dolphin named Cindy. The woman had met Cindy fifteen years before and said it was 'love at first sight.'

I'm not sure what's more disconcerting, the marriage or the fact that someone would name a male dolphin 'Cindy.'

• Associated Press, "With This Herring I Thee Wed," MSNBC.com, Jan. 3, 2006, www.msnbc.msn.com.

FACT: To fight loneliness, one Navy wife in Georgia purchased a mannequin dressed like a sailor in 2005 to stand in for her husband, who was serving at sea. The woman takes the mannequin to dinner, the cinema, and shopping.

If your wife can replace you with a mannequin and be happy, you must be one boring mother fucker.

• "Navy Wife Finds a NewMan-Nequin," MSNBC.com, December 14, 2005, www.msnbc.msn.com.

FACT: A prominent cause of divorce among older Japanese couples is 'retired husband syndrome.' Doctors first described the syndrome when wives began showing irritability, ulcers, rashes, and other stress symptoms when made to manage their recently retired husbands who have nothing to do but bark orders at them all day long.

By the time you read this, 'retired husband syndrome' will have been renamed 'dead retired husband syndrome.'

• "Retired Husband Syndrome," ABC News, January 11, 2006, http://abcnews.go.com.

FACT: Trichotillomania is a behavioural disorder that makes people rip their own hair out, pulling it from the scalp, eyebrows, eyelashes, and more, with bald patches as result.

90 per cent of adult sufferers are women. All of them mothers, I bet.

• "What Is Compulsive Hair Pulling?," Trichotillomania Learning Centre, www.trich.org.

FACT: Chronic skin picking (CSP) is a serious but largely misunderstood human behavioural problem. CSP sufferers obsessively pick, scratch, and rub their skin, often in an attempt to remove small irregularities or perceived imperfections. This behaviour can result in skin discolouration, scarring, or even severe tissue damage.

Chronic nit-picking (CNP) is a serious but largely tolerated human behavioural problem. CNP sufferers obsessively pick, nag, harangue, and correct others, particularly spouses, children, and co-workers, often in an attempt to remove small irregularities or perceived imperfections.

• "What Is Chronic Skin Picking?," Trichotillomania Learning Centre, www.trich.org.

FACT: People who have borderline personality disorder (BPD) suffer from mood instability, troubled personal relationships, and an inability to control their emotions and impulses. BPD affects up to 10 per cent of all patients under psychiatric care.

And about 80 per cent of psychiatrists giving that care.

• Andreas Meyer-Lindenberg,"The Roots of Problem Personalities," Scientific American, April 2009, www.sciam.com.
• "Borderline Personality Disorder," National Institute Of Mental Health, www.nimh.nih.gov.

FACT: Foreign Accent Syndrome (FAS) is an extremely rare brain disorder that causes sufferers to speak involuntarily in a foreign accent. The illness is the result of trauma affecting the area of the brain that controls speech.

I think my chavvy cousin has this. Every once in a while he'll say something that sounds vaguely like English.

• Andrea Canning, "Foreign Accent Syndrome Gives Sufferers an International Sound," ABC News, November 13, 2008, http://abcnews.go.com.

FACT: The rare neurological disorder Alien Hand Syndrome (AHS) causes the sufferer's hands to move independently, without their control over the action. People with AHS have been known to punch or choke themselves and tear at their clothing without meaning to do so, and may even need to use the healthy hand to curb the alien hand. The condition typically arises after trauma to the brain, brain surgery, or stroke.

'Let's all give it up for E.T.!' (audience applauds). That's what I thought Alien Hand Syndrome was.

• "Definition of Alien hand syndrome," Medicine.net, December 15, 2000, www.medterms.com.
• Charles W. Bryant, "How Alien Hand Syndrome Works," HowStuffWorks.com, www.health. howstuffworks.com.
• "Alien Hand Syndrome: Nerve Impulses Can Cause Movement Even When Person Is Unaware," Science Daily, July 17, 2007, www.sciencedaily.com.

FACT: The Bible is the most shoplifted book.

At least the right people are getting it.

• Jerry MacGregor and Marie Prys, 1001 Surprising Things You Should Know about the Bible (Fall River Press, 2006).

F A C T: People with Cotard's syndrome can suffer from a variety of delusions, which range from a belief that they are missing body parts or vital organs to thinking that they are dead, have lost their soul, or do not even exist. The illness is found mostly in individuals with schizophrenia or bipolar disorder.

You have to exist to be able to think you don't exist, DUH! Schizos are stupid.

• J. Pearn and C. Gardner-Thorpe, "Jules Cotard (1840–1889): His Life and the unique syndrome which bears his name," Neurology, May 14, 2002, 1400–1403, www.ncbi.nlm.nih.gov.

F A C T: People who experience Capgras' delusion are convinced that others, usually those closest to them, have been replaced by identical impostors. The condition affects both sexes, but occurs more frequently in women.

Particularly when their husbands make dinner or take the kids to the park without being asked.

• H. D. Ellis and others," Reduced autonomic responses to faces in Capgras delusion," Proceedings, Biological Sciences, July 22, 1997, 1085–1092, www.pubmedcentral.nih.gov.
• "Capgras Syndrome," Disorder Info Sheet, Psychnet.com, www.psychnet-uk.com.

F A C T: Piblokto, or Arctic hysteria, is a mental disorder that affects people living in the Arctic Circle, typically Inuit women. It is marked by frenzied, disturbed behaviour such as uncontrolled screaming, running wildly, or removing one's clothing in frigid weather; memory loss; seizures; and other symptoms reminiscent of epilepsy.

They also drink a shitload of tequila, which doesn't help.

• Emilio F. Moran and Rhonda Gillett-Netting, Human Adaptability: An Introduction to Ecological Anthropology, 2nd ed. (Westview Press, 2000).
• "Arctic Hysteria," Sarah Efron,Journalist, July/August 2003, www.sarahefron.com.

F A C T: Exploding Head Syndrome is a rare phenomenon in which a person approaching deep sleep experiences a loud bang in his head that sounds like a bomb exploding or similarly loud noise. Though the event seems to originate from inside the head, it is an illusion and does no physical damage to its victim.

Exploding Head Syndrome sounds a lot like a hangover.

• "Exploding Head Syndrome," American Sleep Association, September, 2007, www.sleepassociation.org.

 FACT: Body Integrity Identity Disorder, also known as Amputee Identity Disorder, is a psychological condition that causes sufferers to seek amputations for cosmetic reasons: they want their bodies to match the idealised image they have of themselves as amputees.

Doctors are stumped as to the cause of the disorder. They continue the necessary legwork to arm themselves with the facts before they will go out on a limb and theorise about causation, as they are determined not to come up short and have their efforts cut off at the knees.

• "Body Integrity Identity Disorder," Body Integrity Identity Disorder, www.biid.org.

 FACT: A mummified hand has been on display in city hall in Münster, Germany for 400 years. It belonged to a notary who falsely certified a document, and had his hand chopped off as punishment, then displayed as a warning.

You should see the warning to flashers.

• Andrea Schulte-Peevers and others, Lonely Planet Germany, 5th ed. (Lonely Planet, 2007), 583.

 FACT: Flamingo tongue was a common delicacy at Roman feasts.

You can still find it today in Vienna sausages and deviled ham.

• Noel Botham, The Book of Useless Information (Perigee, 2006).

 FACT: In the Satere-Mawe tribe in South America, a boy being initiated into manhood is forced to wear gloves woven with hundreds of bullet ants, whose sting is considered the most painful of any insect. The ants sting the boy until he passes out from pain; if he can be revived, he is considered a true man.

Is he disqualified if he craps himself?

• Alex Levinton, "The 5 Most Horrifying Bugs in the World," Cracked.com, www.cracked.com.
• Steve Backshall, Venom: Poisonous Animals in the Natural World [New Holland Publishers, 2007].

 F A C T: In Britain, placing a postage-stamp bearing the monarch upside-down is considered treason.

Even if she looks better that way?

• Alex Wade, "The World's Strangest Laws," Times Online, August 15, 2007, www.business.timesonline.co.uk.

 F A C T: In France, you are forbidden to name a pig 'Napoleon.'

The French hate redundancy.

• Alex Wade, "The World's Strangest Laws," Times Online, August 15, 2007, www.business.timesonline.co.uk.

 F A C T: By law, a pregnant woman can urinate anywhere she wants in Britain – even, if she so chooses, in a police officer's helmet.

But if she has to go for a number two, she'll need to find a Queen's Guard with the bear skin hat. Gotta wipe, you know.

• Alex Wade, "The World's Strangest Laws," Times Online, August 15, 2007, www.business.timesonline.co.uk.

 F A C T: Masturbation is an offense punishable by decapitation in Indonesia.

Tell me that they at least let you finish.

• Alex Wade, "The World's Strangest Laws," Times Online, August 15, 2007, www.business.timesonline.co.uk.

 F A C T: Drunk driving is handled seriously in El Salvador. In San Salvador, offenders may be sentenced to death by firing squad.

Except that the firing squad soldiers are usually drunk, too, and tend to miss.

• Alex Wade, "The World's Strangest Laws," Times Online, August 15, 2007, www.business.timesonline.co.uk.

F A C T: Male doctors in Bahrain are not legally permitted to look directly at a woman's genitals: they may only examine them with a mirror.

I bet that makes childbirth fun.

• Alex Wade, "The World's Strangest Laws," Times Online, August 15, 2007, www.business. timesonline.co.uk.

F A C T: It is illegal for a taxi in London to carry rabid dogs or corpses.

I hope Keith Richards has his own car.

• Alex Wade, "The World's Strangest Laws," Times Online, August 15, 2007, www.business. timesonline.co.uk.

F A C T: An Australian writer was sentenced to three years in a Thai prison and experienced 'unspeakable suffering' because of a few lines in his self-published novel that were deemed insulting to the monarchy.

The book only sold seven copies. The 'unspeakable suffering' occurred when they read his book aloud to him.

• Grant Peck, "Australian Convicted of Insulting Thai Monarchy," ABC News, January 19, 2009, www.abcnews.go.com.

F A C T: In Lebanon, men are permitted to have sexual intercourse with an animal, but only if it is female.

Sex with a male animal is punishable by death. Only IF you survive the attempt

• Eve Marx, What's Your Sexual IQ? (Citadel Press, 2004), 175.

F A C T: It is against the law in France to sell a doll with a face that is not human.

Which is why no one makes a Sarah Jessica Parker Barbie in France.

• Noel Botham, The Best Book of Useless Information Ever: A Few Thousand Other Things You Probably Don't Need to Know (but Might as Well Find Out) (Perigee, 2007), 46.

F A C T: Donald Duck was once banned in Finland because he doesn't wear any trousers.

Finns, you didn't miss anything.

• Noel Botham, The Best Book of Useless Information Ever: A Few Thousand Other Things You Probably Don't Need to Know (but Might as Well Find Out) (Perigee, 2007), 46.

F A C T: Hindus believe that cow urine is medicinal; it is often drunk in religious festivals.

They'll never run out, that's for sure.

• Matthias Williams, "They Call it Mellow Yellow'?" Reuters, February 12, 2009, www.reuters.com.

F A C T: A fifth of Ireland's towns are at high risk for cryptosporidium infection, a disease spread through drinking water contaminated by human faeces.

But no one ever gets it because it's not found in booze.

• Rose George, The Big Necessity: The Unmentionable World of Human Waste and Why It Matters (St. Martin's Press, 2008).

F A C T: The drive-through line on the opening day of a new McDonald's in Kuwait City reached seven miles long at times.

That's a lot of disappointed people.

• "The McDonald's History – 1994 to Today," McDonald's Corporation, www.mcdonalds.com.

F A C T: In South Korea in 2005, a twenty-eight-year-old man was killed by a heart attack brought on by exhaustion from playing a video game online for fifty hours.

PWNƆD!!!

• "S Korean dies after games session," BBC News, August 10, 2005, www.news.bbc.co.uk.

F A C T: On average, a Chinese person takes his or her own life every two minutes, adding up to 250,000 to 300,000 suicides a year.

Some Chinese like to save the government the trouble.

• Pascale Trouillaud, "Chinese Committing Suicide Every Two Minutes," news.com.au, December 9, 2008, www.news.com.au.

 FACT: In 2005, as many as twelve Iraqi barbers were executed by militant Islamic gangs for shaving men's beards and giving Western-style haircuts.

The ones who gave mullet cuts were executed twice.

• Robert F. Worth, "A Haircut in Iraq Can Be the Death of the Barber," New York Times, March18, 2005, www.nytimes.com.

 FACT: In 2005 Malawi president Binguwa Mutharika fled his home, a 300-bedroom mansion, because he thought that it was haunted.

It wasn't ghosts that he heard in the night, but Madonna, sneaking around looking for more kids to steal.

• "Ghosts Scare off Malawi Leader," BBC News, March,2005, www.news.bbc.co.uk.

 FACT: More than a dozen Nigerian Muslims were sentenced to death by stoning for 'sexual offenses' such as adultery and homosexuality. Many others were flogged by horsewhip for drinking alcohol.

Hopefully they drank enough not to feel anything.

• "Gay Nigerians Face Shari Death," BBC News, August 10, 2007, www.news.bbc.co.uk.

 FACT: Afghanistan passed a new law in 2010 allowing husbands to refuse food to wives who refuse sex.

Brilliant! Either men get laid or their wives lose weight. A win-win.

• "New Afghan Law Does Not allow Marital Rape . . . But Lets Men Refuse to Feed Wives Who Deny Them Sex, Says Cleric," MailOnline, April 17, 2009, www.dailymail.co.uk.

 FACT: In Saudi Arabia, sodomy is considered a legal offense for which you can be sentenced to death.

I'm guessing that there are a lot of things punishable by death in Saudi Arabia.

• Nadya Labi, "The Kingdom in the Closet," The Atlantic Monthly, May 2007, www.theatlantic.com.

 F A C T: An eleven-year-old schoolgirl in New Delhi died at the hands of her teacher in 2009. The student was beaten and forced to stand outside in the hot sun for nearly two hours for her inability to say the English alphabet.

I hope that person was fired.

• "Delhi Girl in Coma after School Punishment Dies," Times of India, April 18, 2009, www.timesofindia.indiatimes.com.

 F A C T: When a flash flood swept a bus into a river near New Delhi in 1973, 78 passengers drowned because they belonged to two separate castes and refused to share a rope that would have saved their lives.

India sounds fun. Let's go there.

• Bruce Felton and Mark Fowler, Felton & Fowler's More Best, Worst, and Most Unusual (New York: Thomas Y. Crowell Company, 1976).

 F A C T: The land that later became the country of Liberia was purchased by the American Colonization Society in 1822. They bought it for a box of beads, several pairs of shoes, soap, some rum, and several spoons, among other things.

They overpaid.

• David Wallechinsky and Irving Wallace, The People's Almanac (Garden City, NY: Doubleday & Company, 1975).

 F A C T: Newborns in parts of northern Spain participate in an annual 'baby-jumping' festival each spring, where a man dressed as the devil leaps over as many as five or six infants on a mattress at a time. The ancient rite is meant to drive away evil spirits.

Because evil spirits might traumatise babies, not unlike a man dressed as the devil leaping over them.

• Editors Of Mental Floss, Mental Floss Presents Instant Knowledge (Harper Collins, 2005).
• "Spanish Village Holds Baby Jump," BBC News, May 25, 2008, www.news.bbc.co.uk.

 FACT: Gloucestershire's annual cheese-rolling contest, where contestants chase a seven-pound circular block of cheese down a steep, bumpy hill, is a dangerous event. Contestants fall, break bones, and have even split their heads open.

Gloucestershire must be really bored.

• Editors of Mental Floss, Mental Floss Presents Instant Knowledge (Harper Collins, 2005).

 FACT: In 2007, a British teacher working in Sudan was arrested and charged with blasphemy for letting a student call their teddy bear 'Mohammed.' The teacher spent fifteen days in jail, but, under Sudanese law, could have been given forty lashes and three months in prison.

There goes my holiday plans. I need somewhere a little less intense. I wonder if North Korea is nice this time of year?

• "Reports: Sudan Arrests UK Teacher for Teddy Bear Blasphemy," CNN.com, November 26, 2007, www.cnn.com.
• "Mohamed Teddy Bear Teacher, Gillian Gibbons, Is Spared Lash but Gets 15 Days in Jail," Times Online, November 30, 2007, www.timesonline.co.uk.

 FACT: In the 1800s, the Chinese considered strangling a less severe punishment than other forms of execution, since the body would not be permanently disfigured.

Because it's important to look your best for the worms.

• Isaac Asimov, ed., Isaac Asimov's Book of Facts (Hastings House, 1979).

 FACT: Dogs are considered food in some regions of East and Southeast Asia. 1 million dogs, 6,000 restaurants, and 10 per cent of the population are involved in the dog meat industry in South Korea.

I wish some dog-eating South Koreans would move to my neighbourhood.

• William Saletan, "Wok the Dog," Slate.com, January 16, 2002, www.slate.com.

F A C T: During famines that ravaged North Korea from 1995 to 1997, starving people would dig up bodies from fresh graves to eat the meat.

If I ever get that hungry, please shoot me. Thanks in advance.

• Doug Struck, "Opening a Window on North Korea's Horrors," Washington Post, October 4, 2003, www.washingtonpost.com.

F A C T: In 2008, Tanzanian witch doctors sanctioned a series of murders in which at least twenty-nine albino children were hacked to death for their body parts, believed by local customs to bring good luck.

Because being an albino wasn't hard enough already.

• Alex Duval Smith, "Albino Africans Live in Fear after Witch-Doctor Butchery," The Observer, November 16, 2008, www.guardian.co.uk.

F A C T: The Parsee, a Zoroastrian sect in India, practise the ancient ritual of 'sky-burial,' where the dead bodies of loved ones are placed on a high stone platform, stripped naked, and left for vultures. Once picked clean, the bones are swept into a deep well.

As delightful as that sounds, I think I'll stick with cremation.

• Tim McGirk, "Shortage of Vultures Threatens Ancient Culture: Many Parsees Are Questioning the Tradition of Sky Burial," The Independent, September 16, 1992, www.independent.co.uk.

F A C T: Every year on the eve of December 5th, St Nicholas Day, Austrians celebrate Krampus Night, when people dress up as Krampus, a demon, and roam the streets looking for incorrigible children to beat with a stick. The tradition is meant to encourage good behaviour in children.

Where do I sign up?

• "Eight Truly Strange Christmas Customs," Mental_Floss, December 11 2008, www.mentalfloss.com.

F A C T: In Spain, a Catalonian Christmas tradition features a statue of a little man pooing as part of the Nativity scene. The entire town of

Bethlehem, Mary, Joseph, and the baby Jesus are depicted – along with the little man, Caganer, doing his business in the corner.

We all get excited about Christmas. Some more than others.

• "Eight Truly Strange Christmas Customs," Mental_Floss, December 11, 2008, www.mentalfloss.com.

 F A C T: In Dutch tradition, Sinterklass (Santa Claus) is accompanied by a slave named Zwarte Piet (Black Pete). Children are warned that if they don't behave, Black Pete might take them back to Spain.

And put them to work cleaning up all the Caganer shit in the Nativity scenes.

• "Eight Truly Strange Christmas Customs," Mental_Floss, December 11, 2008, www.mentalfloss.com.

 F A C T: Ancient custom in Fiji dictated that when a man died, his wives, slaves and friends should all be strangled.

The custom was discontinued when they started running low on Fijians to kill.

• "History Of Funeral Customs," Wisconsin Funeral Directors, www.wyfda.org.

 F A C T: India's Brahmin once practised sati, or wife burning. When her husband died, a widow would dress in her finest clothing and lie with his body on the funeral pyre to be burned alive.

I hope sati isn't the same thing as satay. I've had satay, and come to think of it, it was a little charred.

• Erin McHugh, The 5 W's: Why? An Omnium-Gatherum of World Wars and World Series, Superstitions and Psychoses, the Tooth Fairy Rule and Turkey City Lexicon and Other of Life's Wherefores (Sterling Publishing Company, 2005).
• Jyotsna Kamat, "The Origins of the Sati System," Kamat's Potpourri, www.kamat.com.

 F A C T: Chinese authorities are cracking down on the practise of hiring strippers to perform at funerals. Family and friends hire the women in order to draw more people to a funeral, since many Chinese believe that the larger the crowd, the more luck will come to relatives of the departed.

I've always heard that one should go out with a bang. You won't – you'll be

dead – but maybe your friends will get laid in your honour.

• "Take A Trip Around The World," My Funky Funeral, www.myfunkyfuneral.com.
• "China Acts on Funeral Strippers,"BBC News, August 23, 2006, www.news.bbc.co.uk.

 F A C T: Among some North American Indian groups, a husband has the right to bite or cut off the nose of an adulterous wife.

Her nose isn't the problem.

• George Monger, Marriage Customs of the World: From Henna to Honeymoons (ABC-CLIO, 2004).

 F A C T: Hindu Laws of Manu state that a man should ideally be three times older than his wife; by this standard, the wife of a twenty-four-year-old man should be eight years old.

No bride should have to plan her wedding around Brownie meetings.

• George Monger, Marriage Customs of the World: From Henna to Honeymoons (ABC-CLIO, 2004).

 F A C T: In Samoa, it was once custom for a virgin bride's hymen to be broken publicly by the village chief.

Sometimes the chief was her dad. Awkward.

• George Monger, Marriage Customs of the World: From Henna to Honeymoons (ABC-CLIO, 2004).

 F A C T: Laos, Thailand, and Cambodia are working to build a golf course in the Emerald Triangle, an area where the three countries' borders meet, with nine holes in each country. The only problem: the region is covered with minefields left over from the Vietnam War and other regional conflicts.

'What's your handicap?' 'Both legs below the knee and a hand.'

• Brent W. Ritchie and Daryl Adair, Sport Tourism: Interrelationships, Impacts and Issues (Channel View Publications, 2004).

FACT: Some of the most prestigious libraries in the world have books bound in human skin.

They don't have any skin magazines, though, so don't ask.

• M.L. Johnson, "Some of Nation's Best Libraries Have Books Bound in Human Skin," Boston Globe, January 7, 2006, www.boston.com.

 FACT: Freshly washed towels might smell and look nice, but if they were washed with underwear, they could be contaminated with faeces.

That's the kind of underwear you just throw away, not wash.

• Philip M. Tierno, The Secret Life of Germs: What They Are, Why We Need Them, and How We Can Protect Ourselves Against Them (Simon & Schuster, 2004), 93.

 FACT: A woman had her big toe chewed off by her pet miniature dachshund while sleeping. Because of diabetes-related nerve damage in her extremities, the woman felt nothing and slept through the attack.

Maybe her feet smelled like cheese. Mine sometimes do.

• "'Beloved Dachshund' Chews Off Owner's Toe," Reuters, July 4, 2008, www.news.com.
• "Sausage Dogs Are the Most Aggressive," Telegraph UK, July5, 2008, www.telegraph.co.uk. 951

 FACT: Blood in stool or diarrhoea can be a sign of necrotizing entercolitis, a condition which causes the lining of the intestinal wall to die allowing tissue to fall off. The disease has a death rate of 25 per cent.

Because diarrhoea wasn't fun enough already.

• Jenifer K. Lehrer, "Necrotizing Enterocolitis," Medical Encyclopedia, Medline Plus, U.S. National Library of Medicine and National Institutes of Health, May 3, 2007, www.nlm.nih.gov.

 FACT: In 1970, a dead sperm whale on an Oregon beach was blown up with dynamite in an attempt to get rid of the decomposing corpse. Flying debris from the blast destroyed the roof of a nearby car, and onlookers were covered with whale particles.

Really? Because it sounded like such a good idea.

• "A Brief History of Actual Exploding Animals," WebEcoist, September 5, 2008, www.webecoist.com.

FACT: There are an estimated 27 million slaves in the world today, more than were taken from Africa during the four-century long transatlantic slave trade.

Where the hell are they? My car could do with a wash.

• Andrew Cockburn, "21st Century Slaves," National Geographic, www.ngm.nationalgeographic.com.

 FACT: In one case involving the lethal use of a Taser, a doctor suffered an epileptic seizure after crashing his car, and was repeatedly shocked when he failed to comply with an officer's commands. The seizure was to blame for his lack of response, and the Taser shocks resulted in his death.

Not the policeman's fault. He kept asking him if he wanted another jolt, and the doc kept nodding his head yes.

• "Tasers – Potentially Lethal and Easy to Abuse," Amnesty International report, December 16, 2008, www.amnesty.org.

 FACT: The Amazon's Uape Indians mix their recently cremated relatives' ashes with alcohol to be imbibed by all members of the family as they share fond memories of the deceased.

'Who wants another shot of Grandma?'

• eBizarre, www.ebizarre.com.

 FACT: Two minutes after lethal injection drugs were administered to Raymond Landry during his 1988 execution in Texas, the syringe ejected from his vein, causing deadly chemicals to spray across the room towards witnesses.

Ray wasn't around to see it, unfortunately, and missed all of the excitement.

• Russ Kick, Disinformation Book of Lists: Subversive Facts and Hidden Information in Rapid-fire Format (The Disinformation Company, 2004).

 FACT: In 1535, French Huguenot Antoine Poile had his tongue pierced and attached to his cheek before being burnt alive.

People pay good money for that now. Piercing, that is. Not burning alive.

• Jean Kellaway, The History of Torture and Execution: From Early Civilization through Medieval Times to the Present (Globe Pequot, 2003).

 F A C T: In 1581, writer John Stubs was convicted of sedition for insulting Queen Elizabeth and was sentenced to public mutilation, where his right hand was chopped off and the wound cauterized with a hot iron.

His right arm became known as Stubs' stub.

• Jean Kellaway, The History of Torture and Execution: From Early Civilization through Medieval Times to the Present (Globe Pequot, 2003).

 F A C T: Records show that money lenders in 1124 had their hands and testicles cut off by order of Henry I.

And you thought that 2008 was a bad year for banks.

• Jean Kellaway, The History of Torture and Execution: From Early Civilization through Medieval Times to the Present (Globe Pequot, 2003).

 F A C T: There are four sunken nuclear submarines at the bottom of the Atlantic Ocean. One, located near Bermuda, holds sixteen live nuclear warheads.

No wonder Bermuda's a little uptight.

• Legends of America, www.legendsofamerica.com.

 F A C T: The Iron Maiden was an upright coffin with interior spikes used in medieval torture. The victim was forced inside and, as the door was closed, had his lungs and eyes pierced by the spikes. But the prongs were too short to kill instantly, so the prisoner lingered in agony for hours.

The device is no longer used; now we have the music of Iron Maiden to torture us instead.

• Jean Kellaway, The History of Torture and Execution: From Early Civilization through Medieval Times to the Present (Globe Pequot, 2003).

F A C T: In medieval England, women were punished with the ducking stool, a dangling seat on a rope used to drop them into water. The shock of the cold water and the length of the ducking were often enough to kill.

The good news is that the ducking baptised them as well, so they all went to heaven when they drowned.

• Jean Kellaway, The History of Torture and Execution: From Early Civilization through Medieval Times to the Present (Globe Pequot, 2003).

 F A C T: In sixteenth to nineteenth century England and Scotland, women deemed 'troublesome and angry' could be subjected to the 'scold's bridle,' a metal helmet with a gagging strap that prevented them from speaking.

And...?

• Jean Kellaway, The History of Torture and Execution: From Early Civilization through Medieval Times to the Present (Globe Pequot, 2003).

 F A C T: In Russia during the time of Ivan the Terrible, it was customary for captured highwaymen to have their heels cut off or crushed and be dragged along by their injured ankles.

Okay, but why did they call him Ivan the Terrible?

• Jean Kellaway, The History of Torture and Execution: From Early Civilization through Medieval Times to the Present (Globe Pequot, 2003).

 F A C T: Pressing to death was a form of torture used in fifteenth century England in which the offender was laid naked with a board across his torso. Iron weights were then piled on the board each day, until the pressure was excruciating and often fatal.

I'd take my sandwich and say, 'Hey, do you mind if I stick this in there?' Love those pressed sandwiches.

• Jean Kellaway, The History of Torture and Execution: From Early Civilization through Medieval Times to the Present (Globe Pequot, 2003).

F A C T : As many as 900 people died during witch-hunts in the Lorraine region of France from 1580 to 1595. Some villages cleared of 'witches' were left with just a single female resident.

And she probably liked it. Women can be very competitive.

• Jean Kellaway, The History of Torture and Execution: From Early Civilization through Medieval Times to the Present (Globe Pequot, 2003).

F A C T : In six centuries of church sanctioned witch hunts, an estimated 100,000 people died from torture and being burned at the stake.

That number is probably high, though, so it's not as bad as it sounds.

• Jean Kellaway, The History of Torture and Execution: From Early Civilization through Medieval Times to the Present (Globe Pequot, 2003).

F A C T : Just while making the bed, the average person traverses four miles in a year.

That's one huge bed.

• eBizarre, www.ebizarre.com.

F A C T : Being unmarried can shorten a man's life by ten years.

Being married can shorten it by a lot more.

• eBizarre, www.ebizarre.com.

F A C T : Two thousand years ago, the condemned in the Moche civilization in Peru suffered shockingly brutal execution methods, including being skinned alive, decapitated, drained of blood, or bound tightly and picked to death by vultures.

That's harsh, all right, but I give them points for creativity.

• Jean Kellaway, The History of Torture and Execution: From Early Civilization through Medieval Times to the Present (GlobePequot, 2003).

F A C T : The pillory was a common punishment in colonial America and eighteenth century England and France. Similar to stocks, the pillory held offenders in place as onlookers hit them with rocks, rubbish, food, faeces, dead animals, and more, sometimes to death. In 1756, four Englishmen died after just one hour in the pillory.

That would be fun, actually. To throw stuff, I mean. Not to be in the pillory.

• Jean Kellaway, The History of Torture and Execution: From Early Civilization through Medieval Times to the Present (Globe Pequot, 2003).

 F A C T: In Los Angeles in 1970, authorities discovered 'Genie,' a feral child who had spent ten years locked alone in a room by her abusive father. At thirteen, Genie could barely walk and talk, was not toilet-trained, could not chew solid food, and could not focus her eyes further than twelve feet.

Genie's dad – now there's a guy who needs to be pilloried. I'd bring bricks.

• "Genie: A Modern-Day Wild Child," in Learning About Learning, Great Explorations in Math and Science series from the Lawrence Hall of Science, (The Regents of the University of California), FeralChildren.com, www.feralchildren.com.

 F A C T: A 2009 study revealed that young male children of busy or neglectful parents can feel more closely bonded to characters from the television shows they watch, like Bob the Builder, than their fathers.

Just another reason not to let your kids watch Teletubbies.

• "Boys Develop Closer Bonds with Bob the Builder Than with Parents," Daily Mail, May 25, 2009, www.telegraph.co.uk.

 F A C T: A five-year-old girl nearly died in early 2009 after she had swallowed so much of her own hair that it became a rope-like structure that wrapped around her organs – a condition known as Rapunzel Syndrome.

Hair today, gone tomorrow.

• Luke Salkeld and Alison Smith Squire, "The Real-Life Rapunzel: The Moral of Millie's Grim Tale Is, Don't Chew Your Hair," Daily Mail, May 23, 2009, www.dailymail.co.uk.

 F A C T: Ingested cocaine may lead to severe bowel gangrene caused by reduced blood flow.

Gangrene is defined as 'necrosis or death of soft tissue...usually followed by decomposition and putrefaction,' so the bowels are the ideal place for it.

• "Cocaine," Psychology Today, www.psychologytoday.com.
• "Cocaine," Dictionary.com, www.dictionary.reference.com.

 F A C T: In 2009, a Black Angus calf was born in Colorado with seven legs, two spines, and two hooves on one leg. The calf only survived for ten minutes.

I hope that they ate it. That's a lot of veal.

• "Calf In Colorado Born With 7 Legs, 2 Spines," Steamboat Pilot & Today, May 23, 2009, www.kirotv.com.

 F A C T: One per cent of the entire population in Greenland reside in one apartment building called Blok P.

Luckily, Greenland's population is only like, 100 people, so Blok P is really just a one-bedroom flat.

• eBizarre, www.ebizarre.com.

 F A C T: In 2009, doctors in Izhevsk, Russia found a branch from a fir tree germinated inside the lungs of a man suffering from seizures and coughing up blood.

I say leave it in there, let it grow. He could save some money and be his own Christmas tree.

• "Fir Tree Grows Inside Man's Lungs," Pravda.Ru, April 15, 2009, www.bizarrenews.org.

 F A C T: 'Jigsaw Kid' is the nickname of a six year-old girl born with two left lungs, five spleens, a diseased liver, a hole in her heart, and her stomach on the wrong side. Most of her organs face front-to-back, and when her heart pumps rapidly, you can see it beating through her back.

On the bright side, I'm sure she loves being called 'Jigsaw Kid.' Children aren't sensitive to that sort of thing at all.

• "'Jigsaw Kid' Lives with Jumbled Up Internal Organs," Daily Mail, May 22, 2009, www.telegraph.co.uk.

F A C T: A 2009 study by a leading fossil expert suggests that modern humans hunted and ate Neanderthals, a sturdy species that mysteriously disappeared 30,000 years ago as modern humans migrated to Europe.

We preferred to eat wild boar back then, but Neanderthals were slower.

• Robin McKie, "How Neanderthals Met a Grisly Fate: Devoured by Humans," The Observer, May 17, 2009, www.guardian.co.uk.

 F A C T: A twenty-three-year-old New Zealand mother lost over six stone and suffered a heart attack after drinking nothing but Red Bull – from ten to fourteen cans a day – for eight months.

Her friends call her 'The Great Cornholio,' after the beloved Beavis & Butt-Head character.

• "Traces of Cocaine Found in Red Bull Cola," NEWS.com.au, May 26, 2009, www.news.com.au.

 F A C T: The Vatican started a Facebook page in 2009, gathering 45,000 contacts and 500,000 page views within days of launch.

The 'How Well Do You Know Saint Eusebius of Vercelli?' quiz is a big hit.

• Ariel David, "Vatican Launches Facebook Application," kirotv.com, May 22, 2009, www.kirotv.com.

 F A C T: Medorthophobia is the fear of an erect penis.

It must be a female thing, because men are only afraid of the opposite problem.

• Shane Mooney, Useless Sexual Trivia: Tastefully Prurient Facts about Everyone's Favourite Subject (Simon & Schuster, 2000).

 F A C T: 'Dork' is the proper term for a whale penis, hence the derogatory term.

Calling someone 'whale dick' just doesn't have the same ring to it.

• Shane Mooney, Useless Sexual Trivia: Tastefully Prurient Facts about Everyone's Favourite Subject (Simon & Schuster, 2000).

F A C T: The world's largest mammal, the blue whale, also has the largest penis in the animal kingdom, measuring about ten feet long and a foot in diameter.

I bet it works like a rudder. They can steer with it.

• Shane Mooney, Useless Sexual Trivia: Tastefully Prurient Facts about Everyone's Favourite Subject (Simon & Schuster, 2000).

F A C T: Protein is rare in some parts of Kenya, so natives drink cow's blood for nourishment instead.

I think I'd rather eat a Neanderthal.

• Arkady Leokum and K. R. Hobbie, The Little Giant Book of Weird & Wacky Facts (Sterling Publishing Company, 2005).

F A C T: In August 2007, more than 75,000 Elvis fans descended on Graceland to commemorate the thirtieth anniversary of the singer's death.

Most of them even fatter and on more drugs than Elvis was when he died.

• Varla Ventura, The Book of the Bizarre: Freaky Facts & Strange Stories (Weiser, 2008).

F A C T: Actor Rudolph Valentino's dog reportedly haunts his former owner's gravesite.

Looking for his goddamn dinner.

• Varla Ventura, The Book of the Bizarre: Freaky Facts & Strange Stories (Weiser, 2008).

F A C T: In the fifth century, castration was believed to cure the plague.

It worked, too. The disease disappeared among men virtually overnight.

• Shane Mooney, Useless Sexual Trivia: Tastefully Prurient Facts about Everyone's Favourite Subject (Simon & Schuster, 2000).

F A C T: Capuchin monkeys often greet each other by showing off their erections.

My dog does the same thing, but you have to stroke him first.

• Shane Mooney, Useless Sexual Trivia: Tastefully Prurient Facts about Everyone's Favourite Subject (Simon & Schuster, 2000).

F A C T: An iceberg spotted by the U.S. Coast Guard in 1956 was roughly the size of Belgium.

And probably a lot more interesting.

• Barbara Seuling, Earth Is Likea Giant Magnet: And Other Freaky Facts About Planets, Oceans, and Volcanoes (Coughlan Publishing, 2007).

 F A C T: Queen Isabella of Spain lived to be fifty years old, but bathed just twice in her lifetime.

She was so dirty, that even the flies refused to land on her. Even dirt wouldn't stick to her. When she walked past a pigpen, all the pigs would hold their noses.

• eBizarre, www.ebizarre.com.

 F A C T: In the past ten years the 'naked recreation and travel' industry has grown by 233 per cent.

And that's just the erections.

• eBizarre, www.ebizarre.com.

 F A C T: Until the late 1800s, Turkish women suspected of committing adultery were put in bags with live cats and thrown into the sea.

Getting rid of the cats was just an added bonus.

• Varla Ventura, The Book of the Bizarre: Freaky Facts & Strange Stories. Weiser, 2008.

 F A C T: The longest case of hiccups on record lasted sixty-nine years.

That's one patient man. I think I'd throw myself off a bridge after 69 hours.

• Katharine Kenah, The Bizarre Body (School Specialty Publishing, 2004).

 F A C T: Collectively, Americans spend 250 billion hours watching television every year. If spent working for a $5 per hour wage, this time would be worth $1.25 trillion.

I don't think five bucks an hour is enough to pull anybody away from the TV.

• "Television & Health: Television Statistics," Compiled byTV-Free America, www.csun.edu.

 FACT: When polled, more than half of four- to six-year-olds picked watching television over spending time with their fathers.

Probably because spending time with your dad usually involves being put to work in some way.

• "Television & Health: Television Statistics," Compiled byTV-Free America, www.csun.edu.

 FACT: By the time they finish elementary school, American children have seen 8,000 murders on TV. By the time they graduate from high school, they witness 200,000 violent acts and 40,000 murders.

Or you can just save him some time and let him watch the movie 300.

• "Television & Health: Television Statistics," Compiled byTV-Free America, www.csun.edu.

 FACT: In 2004, students at Alexandria Country Day School got a surprise with their lunch: cafeteria workers accidentally served them pre-mixed margaritas left over from a staff party, mistaking it for limeade.

Unlike the staff, the students kept their clothes on. Like the staff, several of them puked.

• Valerie Strauss, "'Limeade' Packs a Punch," Washington Post, September 29, 2004, www.washingtonpost.com.

 FACT: A 1999 Gallup poll revealed that one in five Americans believes that the sun orbits the Earth.

Wait – it doesn't?

• Steve Crabtree, "New Poll Gauges Americans' General Knowledge Levels," Gallup, www.gallup.com.

 FACT: Less than 50 per cent of American adults comprehend that the Earth revolves around the sun on a yearly basis.

These are the same people who think that Elvis is alive and Bigfoot is real, so you can't really be surprised.

• Steve Crabtree, "New Poll Gauges Americans' General Knowledge Levels," Gallup, www.gallup.com.
• Peter Strupp and Alan Dingman, Fat, Dumb, and Ugly: The Decline of the Average American (Simon & Schuster, 2004).

 F A C T: In a poll conducted by Newsweek in 2007, 41 per cent of Americans continued to believe that Saddam Hussein's Iraqi regime planned, financed, or carried out the September 11th, 2001 terrorist attacks. The majority of people polled did not know that most of the 9/11 hijackers hailed from Saudi Arabia.

I would expect no less from people who believe that pork is the 'other white meat' and Budweiser is 'premium' beer.

• Joerg Wolf, "More Americans Believe that Saddam Was Directly Involved in 9/11," Atlantic Review, June 27, 2007, www.atlanticreview.org.

 F A C T: In 1992, Nike paid Michael Jordan $2 million to promote their shoes, as much money as the combined wages of all the workers in the factories that made them.

But they all got free Nike 'swoosh' headbands, which really help control the sweat on that three hour walk to and from work every day.

• Diana Elizabeth Kendall and others, Sociology in Our Times,2nd ed. (Nelson Thomson Learning,1999).

 F A C T: 35 per cent of Americans eat at a fast food restaurant at least once a week. And then 99 per cent of them race home to take a dump.

The other 1 per cent can't wait that long and have the added delight of going right there in Burger King. Or crapping their pants, which might actually be preferable.

• "Consumers in Europe – Our Fast Food/Take Away Consumption Habits," AC Nielsen, 2004, www.ie.nielsen.com.

F A C T: In its first year at sea, dozens of seats on the newly launched luxury cruise liner, the Queen Mary 2, collapsed when obese American passengers sat down on them.

They weren't obese when the cruise started.

• Olinka Koster, "QM2 Chairs Buckle Under Weighty Cruisers," Daily Mail, www.dailymail.co.uk.

F A C T: The obesity rate in the United States doubled from 1988 to 2002. Approximately 65 per cent of adult Americans are either obese or overweight.

But they all intend to lose it. No, really. They're getting a treadmill.

• "Prevalence of Overweight and Obesity Among Adults: United States, 1999–2002,"National Centre for Health Statistics, Centres for Disease Control and Prevention, www.cdc.gov.

F A C T: . The newborn mortality rate in America is more than twice that of Finland, Iceland, or Norway. The only developed country in the world where the newborn death rate surpasses the United States is Latvia.

You can't really blame anyone for not wanting to be Latvian.

• Jeff Green, "U.S. Has Second Worst Newborn Death Rate in Modern World, Report Says," CNN, May 10, 2006, www.cnn.com.

F A C T: About 14 per cent of Americans between eighteen and twenty-four cannot find Iraq on a map, and 18 per cent can't find Afghanistan.

Which is why the Army recruits from that age group.

• Peter Strupp and Alan Dingman Fat, Dumb, and Ugly: The Decline of the Average American (Simon & Schuster, 2004).

F A C T: Ten per cent of Americans between eighteen and twenty-four can't find the United States on a blank world map.

Shhh, I'm watching The Hills!

• Peter Strupp and Alan Dingman Fat, Dumb, and Ugly: The Decline of the Average American (Simon & Schuster, 2004).

F A C T: Twenty-eight million Americans use indoor tanning booths every year. Perhaps it is no coincidence, then, that the per capita rate for melanoma has increased by 100 per cent in the last thirty years.

Well, tanning beds do look a lot like coffins.

• Peter Strupp and Alan Dingman, Fat, Dumb, and Ugly: The Decline of the Average American (Simon & Schuster, 2004).

 F A C T: Just five days before the 2008 election, 23 per cent of Texans still believed – erroneously – that Barack Obama was Muslim.

I could write an entire chapter on stupid things that Texans believe.

• Richard S. Dunham, "UT Poll Shows McCain, Cornyn with Comfortable Margins," Houston Chronicle, October 29, 2008, www.chron.com.

 F A C T: A majority of Americans don't know that they are the only country that has used nuclear weapons in war.

Many Americans can't even pronounce 'nuclear,' so, once again, not surprising.

• Rick Shenkman, Just How Stupid Are We?: Facing the Truth About the American Voter (Public Affairs, 2009).

 F A C T: The Strategic Task Force on Education Abroad assessed Americans' knowledge of world affairs in 2003, concluding that 'America's ignorance of the outside world' is a 'national liability' that creates a threat to our security.

Not to be confused with The Strategic Ass Force on Educatin' A Broad.

• Rick Shenkman, Just How Stupid Are We?: Facing the Truth About the American Voter (Public Affairs, 2009).
• Burton Bollag, "Report Urges Federal Effort to Triple Number of Students Studying Abroad," Institute Of International Education, Chronicle of Higher Education, November 21, 2003, www.opendoors.iienetwork.org.

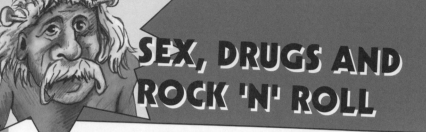

SEX, DRUGS AND ROCK 'N' ROLL

Taking the fun out of... everything

 F A C T: 35 per cent of people who use dating websites are married.

Hey, we all forget things sometimes.

• Bernice Kanner, Are You Normal about Sex, Love, and Relationships? (Macmillan, 2004).

 F A C T: Only 15 per cent of sexually active adults have been tested for HIV, says the National Centre for Health Statistics. The other 85 per cent are certain they don't have it.

No, really, there's no way they could possibly have it, so why bother with that annoying condom?

• Bernice Kanner, Are You Normal about Sex, Love, and Relationships? (Macmillan, 2004).

 F A C T: 12 per cent of men surveyed say they would not tell a partner if they were HIV-positive.

At least not until after they've had sex. That would just kill the mood.

• Bernice Kanner, Are You Normal about Sex, Love, and Relationships? (Macmillan, 2004).

 F A C T: Eight per cent of people admit to having sex with a cousin, and six per cent confess to doing it with a sibling or half sibling.

Hard to say what's more troubling: the fact that they do it or that they admit it.

• Bernice Kanner, Are You Normal about Sex, Love, and Relationships? (Macmillan, 2004).

 F A C T: 14 per cent of people admit to having slept with a friend's lover behind his (or her) back.

The trick is to be very quiet and pray he doesn't roll over.

• Bernice Kanner, Are You Normal about Sex, Love, and Relationships? (Macmillan, 2004).

 F A C T: Although the penis is not a bone, it can still be fractured. A fracture can occur when the erect penis endures blunt trauma during sexual intercourse or other physical activity. A cracking sound can be heard, followed by pain and swelling that causes the shape of the penis to become distorted. Surgery is often required to repair the damage.

Every man reading this just clenched his legs together.

• Klemen Jagodic and others, "A Case of Penile Fracture with Complete Urethral Disruption during Sexual Intercourse: A Case Report," Journal of Medical Case Reports, May 2, 2007, www.medicalnewstoday.com

 F A C T: Some women are allergic to their male partner's semen, a condition known as human seminal plasma hypersensitivity. Sufferers complain of symptoms such as wheezing, itching, hives, swelling, chest tightness, vomiting, and diarrhoea. Severe reactions can cause loss of consciousness and even death from anaphylactic shock.

God, don't tell my wife about this condition. She's just looking for an excuse.

• Charles Downey, "Could You Be Allergic to Sex?," Swedish Medical Centre, May 13, 2008, www.swedish.org

 F A C T: We've all heard the jokes, but sexual headaches are a real illness that affects about one in 100 people, either as a dull ache in the neck and head that builds with sexual excitement, or as a sudden and/or severe headache during orgasm.

Don't tell my wife about this one, either.

• Mayo Clinic Staff, "Sex Headaches," Mayo Foundation for Medical Education and Research, Feb. 21, 2008, www.mayoclinic.com.

 F A C T: Yeast infections aren't just a problem for women; men can get them, too, as a result of prolonged antibiotic use, diabetes, an impaired immune system, or, in rare cases, from unprotected sex with a partner who has a yeast infection.

But men already scratch their crotch all the time, so no big deal.

• Michael A. Sommers, Yeast Infections, Trichomoniasis, and Toxic Shock Syndrome (Rosen Publishing Group, 2007).
• "Male Yeast Infections," Mayo Clinic, www.mayoclinic.com.

 F A C T: Overweight men are more likely to have poor semen quality.

But fat guy sperm are jovial and mischievous, and always good for a laugh.

• Associated Press, "Another Reason to Watch Your Waist: Bad Sperm," MSNBC.com, July 9, 2008, www.msnbc.msn.com.

 F A C T: Andropause, a male form of menopause, can affect men over forty. The condition, which can affect mood, memory, and overall health, is marked by a decline in testosterone production, as well as fatigue, depression, and sexual problems.

Some call these conditions 'being over forty.'

• Bernice Kanner, Are You Normal about Sex, Love, and Relationships? (Macmillan, 2004).
• "Low Testosterone Could Kill You," ABC News, June 6, 2007, http://abcnews.go.com.
• Eric R. Braverman, Younger You: Unlock the Hidden Power of Your Brain to Look and Feel 15 Years Younger (McGraw-Hill Professional, 2006).
• "Male Menopause," Cleveland Clinic, www.my.clevelandclinic.org.

 F A C T: Some men can experience retrograde ejaculation, or 'dry orgasms,' when semen travels backwards into the bladder instead of being expelled. The illness can be congenital, or caused by medications, diabetes, or damage to nerves and muscles that control the opening of the bladder. It isn't harmful, but it can cause male infertility.

You'd think that any orgasm would be good. You'd be wrong.

• "Richard D. McAnulty and M. Michele Burnette, Sex and Sexuality: Sexual Function and Dysfunction (Greenwood PublishingGroup, 2006).
• "Retrograde Ejaculation," Mayo Clinic, www.mayoclinic.com.

F A C T: Sexual dysfunction, which includes erectile dysfunction, premature ejaculation, dyspareunia (vaginal pain during intercourse), low sexual desire, and other conditions, occurs in 31 per cent of men and 43 per cent of women.

Men, if you experience vaginal pain during intercourse, talk to your gynecologist. Or a psychiatrist.

• Glen O. Gabbard, Judith S. Beck and Jeremy Holmes, Oxford Textbook of Psychotherapy (Oxford University Press, 2007).

F A C T: Premature ejaculation is the most commonly reported sexual dysfunction in men, affecting one in five. Some researchers attribute the problem to unhealthy masturbation habits and sexual insecurities.

Don't confuse premature ejaculation with premature evacuation – being so nervous about sex that you crap yourself.

• Glen O. Gabbard, Judith S. Beck and Jeremy Holmes, Oxford Textbook of Psychotherapy (Oxford University Press, 2007).

F A C T: A recent study comparing the effectiveness of oral contraceptives as they relate to bodymass index (BMI) shows that obese or overweight women are up to 70 per cent more likely to experience contraception failure and resulting pregnancy than women of average weight.

Fortunately, obese people have the most effective contraceptive of all: obesity.

• Larissa R. Brunner Huber and Jessica L. Toth, "Obesity and Oral Contraceptive Failure: Findings from the 2002 National Survey of Family Growth," American Journal of Epidemiology, June 29, 2007, http://contraception.about.com.

F A C T: Keeping a condom in your wallet is a bad idea. The constant friction and temperature changes can create microscopic tears in the condom that allow sperm to get through.

No one who carries a condom in his wallet should be procreating anyway, at least not until he finishes school.

• David Zieve, Greg Juhn, and David R. Eltz, "Condoms," Medline Plus, U.S. National Library of Medicine, February 19, 2008, www.nlm.nih.gov.

 FACT: The sudden appearance of a sexually transmitted disease (STD) in a monogamous couple does not necessarily indicate infidelity by either partner. Some infections can lie dormant for years after initial exposure.

That's what I told my wife right before she hit me. I guess she wasn't convinced.

• Lois White and Gena Duncan, Medical-Surgical Nursing: An Integrated Approach, 2nd ed. (Cengage Learning, 2002).

 FACT: Persistent Sexual Arousal Syndrome (PSAS) is a medical condition where a woman experiences 'spontaneous, intrusive and unwanted' feelings of arousal in the genital area without sexual desire. PSAS can continue for days or months, is not abated by sexual activity, and causes distraction and psychological distress in sufferers.

Congratulations, ladies. Now you know what it's like to be a man.

• Sandra Leiblum, "About PSAS," Persistent Sexual Arousal Syndrome, www.psas.dreamhosters.com.
• "Medical Mystery: Persistent Sexual Arousal Syndrome." ABC News, February 21, 2008, http://abcnews.go.com.

 FACT: Human males – like rats, moths, and butterflies – give off a scent that has a physiological and psychological effect on the opposite sex. Researchers discovered that androstadienone, a chemical found in male sweat, raises levels of the hormone cortisol in women, resulting in enhanced mood and sexual arousal.

My wife does get pretty excited when she sees a moth.

• "Male sweat boosts women's hormone levels," Physorg.com, February 7, 2007, www.physorg.com.

 FACT: According to one researcher, women have a higher likelihood than men to settle for a mediocre sex life and unmet emotional needs. Most keep their dissatisfaction a secret from their partners, often due to a fear of emotional hurt or abandonment.

Mediocre sex is better than no sex at all, isn't it? That's what I tell my wife.

• Jeanna Bryner, "Women Settle for Mediocre Sex, Scientist Finds," Live Science, AOL Health, February 14, 2007, www.reference.aol.com.

 F A C T: Use of an oral contraceptive might affect a woman's ability to sniff out a partner. In a study where women were asked to sniff men's sweaty shirts, those on the pill typically chose odours that were genetically similar to their own as being the most attractive. Human beings are inclined to go for genetically dissimilar mates.

Obviously, this doesn't apply to those people who admitted having sex with their cousins.

• Jeanna Bryner, "Genetic Test Could Reveal A Cheating Heart," LiveScience, AOL Health, February 13, 2007, www.reference.aol.com.
• "The Facts of Life: Attraction," The Independent, September 13, 2008, www.independent.co.uk.

 F A C T: Several traditional herbs are being studied for their aphrodisiac properties, including yohimbe, tribulus, and maca. Combinations of these are sold as 'natural Viagra,' but be wary: their effectiveness is unproven, and some, like yohimbe, a type of tree bark, can be lethal if consumed in large quantities.

Tree bark? Dude – spring for the Viagra.

• "Top 10 Aphrodisiacs,"LiveScience, AOL Health, www.reference.aol.com.

 F A C T: The average size of an erect penis is five inches, while the average flaccid penis is three and a half inches. Drugs and devices advertised to increase penis size are dismissed as scams.

But you can't blame a guy with a three-inch dong for trying.

• Rob Baedeker, "Sex: Fact And Fiction," WebMD, www.men.webmd.com.

 F A C T: While a penis pump can be an effective treatment for erectile dysfunction, a pump will not permanently increase the size of your organ. In fact, a penis pump can cause numbness and permanent damage if improperly used.

If I were a penis pump manufacturer, I'd try to use the hit song, 'Pump Up The Jam,' in my commercials, except I'd change it to 'Pump Up The Ham.' I think that would be memorable and sell a lot of pumps.

• "Penis Pumps for Erectile Dysfunction: Improve Your Sexual Function," Mayo Clinic, www.mayoclinic.com

FACT: During World War I, the French recorded more than 1 million cases of syphilis and gonorrhea, and Britain suffered a loss of 23,000 men on average for seven-week hospital stays due to STDs.

Well, the French are known as lovers. I'm not sure what got into us.

• Allan M. Brandt, No Magic Bullet: A Social History of Venereal Disease in the United States Since 1880 (Oxford University Press, 1987).

FACT: 'Beer goggles' aren't just a myth: People do appear more attractive after a drink, according to researchers at the University of Bristol. Students who had consumed alcohol rated pictures of people their own age as being more attractive than did participants who had no alcohol.

Booze: helping ugly people get laid since the dawn of time.

• "The Facts of Life: Attraction," The Independent, September 13, 2008, www.independent.co.uk.

FACT: Wearing too much makeup can mask the scent that attracts men to women during ovulation. An experiment found that a woman's armpit scent was at its most attractive to men between the end of her cycle and ovulation, but that this smell is easily obscured by cosmetics.

Trying to describe when an armpit scent is at its most attractive is like trying to say when vomit is at its tastiest.

• "The Facts of Life: Attraction," The Independent, September 13, 2008, www.independent.co.uk.

FACT: Not all people are attracted to other humans. There are believed to be around forty objectum sexuals in the world who feel attraction, arousal, love, and even commitment for an object instead of another person. Swede Eija-RiittaBerliner-Mauer, for example, has been 'married' to the Berlin Wall since 1979.

Nobody has the heart to tell her that they tore it down.

• "The Facts of Life: Attraction," The Independent, September 13, 2008, www.independent.co.uk.

 F A C T: According to a study in Wales, sexual activity seems to have a preventative affect on male health. In several southern Welsh villages, risk for mortality was 50 per cent lower for men with higher frequency of orgasm.

I'm telling my wife about this.

• "Sex and Death: Are They Related? Findings from the Caerphilly Cohort Study," BMJ, December 20, 1997, www.bmj.com.

 F A C T: Traumatic Masturbatory Syndrome (TMS) is the habit of masturbating in a face-down position against a bed or floor, which puts excessive pressure on the penis, and can interfere with sexual relations. The most common problems TMS sufferers have are inorgasmia – inability to reach orgasm during intercourse – or delayed orgasm.

Many TMS sufferers also experience erectile dysfunction. TMI.

• "Facts about Traumatic Masturbatory Syndrome," Healthy Strokes, www.healthystrokes.com.

 F A C T: Many popular antidepressants, particularly selective serotonin reuptake inhibitor medications like Zoloft, Prozac, and Paxil, can lower libido and prevent orgasm.

But then, depression isn't exactly an aphrodisiac.

• "Can Antidepressants Affect Orgasm?" Ask Dr. Laura Berman, Everyday Health, www.everydayhealth.com

 F A C T: More than half of the women surveyed by Shere Hite in 1994 admitted faking orgasm, while fewer than half reported being brought to orgasm by a male partner through intercourse.

I have no problems with a fake orgasm as long she sells it.

• "Eleven Key Things About Orgasms," The Observer, February 11, 2001, www.observer.guardian.co.uk.

F A C T: Masturbation was considered a sin in the late 1800s and early 1900s. Before the 1960s, excessive masturbation was thought to be a mental condition, a fixation on immature or undesirable behaviour that led to adult sexual dysfunction.

It's probably still a sin, but nobody cares anymore.

• "Masturbation: Techniques and Tips For Men And Women," Sexual Health Resource, www.sexual-health-resource.org.

 F A C T: On any given day, about 400 million people across the globe will have sexual intercourse, which means that about 4,000 people are probably having sex right now.

Sadly, I am not one of them. Don't laugh – neither are you.

• "Ten Strange Sex Facts," Seduction Labs, www.seductionlabs.org.

 F A C T: The sexually transmitted disease chlamydia is caused by the bacterium Chlamydia trachomatis. Symptoms of chlamydia are usually mild, but serious cases can lead to irrevocable damage to the reproductive organs, chronic pelvic pain, and infertility, without a woman ever recognizing the problem.

That's two more votes for masturbation.

• "Sexually Transmitted Diseases: HPV," Centres For Disease Control And Prevention, www.cdc.gov.

 F A C T: As much as 6 per cent of the world's population – more than 400million people – suffer from addiction to sex.

Probably the same 400 million who got it on today.

• "Sex Addiction," SexHelp.com, www.sexhelp.com.

 F A C T: Finger holes in bowling balls have been found to contain 'substantial' amounts of faecal contamination.

Pooing into those little holes isn't easy, either, believe me. But when you gotta go, you gotta go.

• Philip M. Tierno, The Secret Life of Germs: What They Are, Why We Need Them, and How we Can Protect Ourselves Against Them (Simon & Schuster, 2004) 108.

F A C T: The game 'hot cockles' was very popular around Christmas in medieval times. It entailed taking turns striking a blindfolded player, who had to guess the name of the person who was doing the hitting.

I usually dread my mother-in-law's Christmas visit, but that just changed. Who wants to play a fun game?'

• Noel Botham, The Best Book of Useless Information Ever: A Few Thousand Other Things You Probably Don't Need to Know (but Might as Well Find Out) (Perigee, 2007).

 F A C T: The severity of sports-related injury increases with age.

The severity of a lot of things increases with age.

• "Sports Injury Statistics," Children's Hospital Boston, www.childrenshospital.org.

 F A C T: Before puberty, girls and boys suffer the same risk of sports injuries, but during puberty, boys suffer more injuries, and more severe injuries, than girls.

Probably because during puberty, boys are trying harder than ever to impress those girls.

• "Sports Injury Statistics," Children's Hospital Boston, www.childrenshospital.org.

 F A C T: Boxers and participants in violent team sports often suffer very high incidence of permanent injuries, disabilities, alcoholism, drug abuse, obesity, and heart problems.

Really? Because Muhammad Ali seems just fine to me.

• Sara L. Crawley, Lara J. Foley, and Constance L. Shehan, Gendering Bodies (Rowman & Littlefield, 2007), 187.

 F A C T: In Ancient Greece, boxing was a more brutal sport than it is today. Fighters wore leather straps to protect their fists, and the contest did not end until one of the fighters was unconscious or dead.

Yes, that sounds totally different from modern boxing. Wait. No, it doesn't.

• "The Most Brutal," Ancient Sports, www.Ancientsports.net.
• Waldo E. Sweet and Erich Segal, Sport and Recreation in Ancient Greece: A Sourcebook with Translations (Oxford University Press, 1987).

F A C T: In boxing, a 'knockout' is synonymous with cerebral concussion, which can lead to short- or even long-term amnesia and confusion. Another concern is that the neurological damage is cumulative and makes the boxer increasingly vulnerable to future injury and permanent neurological trauma.

Amnesia might not be a bad thing, in this case. Who wants to remember getting his arse kicked?

• Julian E. Bailes and Arthur L. Day, Neurological Sports Medicine: A Guide for Physicians and Athletic Trainers (Thieme, 2001).

F A C T: Another popular violent sport in ancient Greece was pankration, a hybrid of wrestling and boxing with no protective gear and no rules, save a ban on gouging of eyes and biting.

We still have this. It's called the Ultimate Fighting Championship. But I think they allow biting and eye-gouging now. And wedgies.

• "The Most Brutal," Ancient Sports, www.ancientsports.net.
• Waldo E. Sweet, Erich Segal, Sport and Recreation in Ancient Greece: A Sourcebook with Translations (Oxford University Press, 1987).

F A C T: Ancient Egyptian sports were brutal. In Fishermen's Jousting, teams of fishermen would knock their opponents out of their boats. Since many fishermen were unable to swim, drownings often resulted.

Because the best sport for people who can't swim is one where they try to knock each other off paper boats into the water.

• "The Most Brutal," Ancient Sports, www.ancientsports.net.
• Steve Craig, Sports and Games of the Ancients (Greenwood Publishing Group, 2002).

F A C T: Chariot racing in ancient Rome was brutal. Drivers wrapped the reins of the chariot around their arms and could not let go if they crashed, allowing them to be dragged behind their horses unless they could free themselves. Many charioteers carried small knives for this purpose.

Then they realised a better solution: find a new hobby. One that doesn't involve chariots.

• "The Most Brutal," Ancient Sports, www.ancientsports.net.

• Eckart Köhne, Cornelia Ewigleben, and Ralph Jackson, Gladiators and Caesars: The Power of Spectacle in Ancient Rome (University of California Press, 2000).

 F A C T: Spanish bullfights are a gruesome tradition. Picadors (lance-yielding men on blindfolded horses) and banderilleros (men on foot who wield sticks with harpoon points) stab a bull in the back and neck. When the bull is weakened, the matador forces a few charges from the bull for show, then kills it with a sword and cuts off the ears or tail as a trophy.

Well that sounds like fun. I must take the children.

• "What is wrong with bullfighting?" League Against Cruel Sports, www.league.org.uk.

 F A C T: Six people died in bullfights in 2004.

What a shame. That there weren't more.

• "What is wrong with bullfighting?" League Against Cruel Sports, www.league.org.uk.

 F A C T: Since 1924, thirteen people have been killed in Pamplona, Spain's annual 'Running of the Bulls' at the San Fermin festival. Injuries have persisted in recent years despite the government's attempts to make the event safer by coating the streets with a special anti-slip paint.

One year, instead of anti-slip paint, they covered the street with butter and banana peels just for fun. The number of injuries increased a bit.

• Damien Simonis, Susan Forsyth, and John Noble, Spain, 6th ed. (Lonely Planet, 2007)

 F A C T: Scuba divers who ascend too quickly also risk decompression sickness, or 'the bends,' which occurs when nitrogen that builds in tissues during the dive is forced back into the blood stream too quickly, resulting in nitrogen bubbles in the blood. The condition is extremely painful and potentially fatal.

Like any of this will matter the next time you're diving and a fifteen-foot shark starts circling.

• "Decompression Symptoms: The Bends," eMedicineHealth, www.emedicinehealth.com.
• Bruce Iliff, "The Bends In Scuba Diving," suite101.com, www.suite101.com.

F A C T: One study showed that over half of sports-related catastrophic spinal cord injuries resulted from diving accidents, most of them during unsupervised or unsponsored activities in which alcohol was a factor.

'Hey! Watch this!'

• Randolph W. Evans, Neurology and Trauma 2nd ed. (Oxford University Press, 2006).

F A C T: Stingers are injuries to the nerves in the neck and shoulder that cause painful electric sensations to radiate through one of the arms. If not properly diagnosed and treated, stingers, which are usually sports-related, can lead to persistent pain and permanent nerve damage.

They might want to rethink that name. Talk about an understatement.

• "The Stinger," North American Spine Society Public Education Series, North American Spine Society, 2006, www.spine.org.

F A C T: From 1973 to 1975, there were eighty-one known fatalities from hang-gliding, usually involving massive head, neck, and chest trauma that included shattered skulls and ruptured aortas, heart lacerations, and pulmonary collapse. The majority of injured hang-gliders arrived at the hospital deceased. Of thirty-seven fatal injuries, 20 per cent involved alcohol.

Alcohol and hang-gliding – great idea!

• Julian E. Bailes and Arthur L. Day, Neurological Sports Medicine: A Guide for Physicians and Athletic Trainers (Thieme, 2001).

F A C T: Rowing is a taxing sport with a significant incidence of injury among participants, ranging from spondylolysis, a stress fracture to one of the vertebrae, to disc disease, chronic pain from a damaged disc. Both conditions can lead to other injuries and degeneration in the spine.

Row, row, row your boat, Paddles in a line, Push 'em up, pull 'em back, Snap your goddamn spine.

• "Spondylolys is and Spondylolisthesis,"American Academy of Orthopaedic Surgeons, www.orthoinfo. aaos.org.
• "Degenerative Disc Disease," Cedars-Sinai Medical Centre, www.csmc.edu.
• Julian E. Bailes and Arthur L. Day, Neurological Sports Medicine: A Guide for Physicians and Athletic Trainers (Thieme, 2001).

F A C T: Skiing carries a high risk of injury to the nervous system that can result in quadriplegia and death. Recreational skiers can easily reach speeds of up to 40 mph when travelling downhill, which can lead to injuries similar to those seen in car accidents.

If you don't believe it, ask Sonny Bono. Oh, wait, hang on a minute...

• Julian E. Bailes and Arthur L. Day, Neurological Sports Medicine: A Guide for Physicians and Athletic Trainers (Thieme, 2001).

F A C T: The use of trampolines carries a great risk for catastrophic injury. In one study, thirty-two out of fifty instances of spinal cord injury in gymnastics involved trampolines.

Still, they're a lot safer now than when I was a child. We didn't have safety nets or spring covers, and the trampolines were made of asbestos, covered in lead paint, and often surrounded by a ring of fire or piranha-filled water or land mines. I saw a lot of good kids go down.

• Julian E. Bailes and Arthur L. Day, Neurological Sports Medicine: A Guide for Physicians and Athletic Trainers (Thieme, 2001).

F A C T: Golf may be considered a benign sport, but it carries risk of injury and death, most often from lightning, power lines, heart attack, and heat stroke. Other deaths have occurred from freak injuries. In one instance, an angry golfer killed his caddie by swinging a club at him after missing a shot, and another player broke his club on a tree, only to have it rebound and impale him.

No one who has played golf considers it a benign sport.

• Julian E. Bailes and Arthur L. Day, Neurological Sports Medicine: A Guide for Physicians and Athletic Trainers (Thieme, 2001).

F A C T: In the United States, at least seven fatalities and numerous severe injuries have been reported among bungee jumpers using a hot airballoon as a platform. In two instances, no one noticed that the balloon lost altitude, making the jump cord too long, and the jumpers hit the ground.

Oops. I hope they got a refund.

• Julian E. Bailes and Arthur L. Day, Neurological Sports Medicine: A Guide for Physicians and Athletic Trainers (Thieme, 2001).

F A C T: The narrowing or obstruction of main arteries supplying blood to the brain stem, or cerebellum, causes Bow-hunter's stroke. This can be caused by forcibly turning your head to one side, commonly on a head rotation of 90 degrees or more to the left, as an archer does when aiming.

The most common cause of death during archery remains the same as always: letting someone try to shoot an apple off the top of your head.

• Julian E. Bailes and Arthur L. Day, Neurological Sports Medicine: A Guide for Physicians and Athletic Trainers (Thieme, 2001).

F A C T: No one would consider lawn darts dangerous – unless they knew that the sport had been associated with skull-penetrating injuries, half of which cause permanent neurological impairment. In fact, the head is the most common body part to sustain injury, usually in children.

Of course it is. Head shots are worth fifty points, plus an extra ten if you hit them in the face.

• Randolph W. Evans, Neurology and Trauma, 2nd ed. (Oxford University Press, 2006).

F A C T: Injuries in equestrian sports are almost twenty times more common than injuries in motorcycling.

Except when you're thrown from a horse you don't bounce off the windscreen of a car or skid down the road on your face.

• Randolph W. Evans, Neurology and Trauma, 2nd ed. (Oxford University Press, 2006).

F A C T: Children spend more time watching TV than all other activities, except sleep.

Do you know what babysitters charge these days?

• Huston and Wright, "Television and Socialization of Young Children," in Tuning In to Young Viewers, ed. T. MacBeth (Thousand Oaks, CA: Sage, 1996), 37–60.

F A C T: Each year about 50–70 confirmed shark attacks and 5–15 shark attack fatalities occur around the world.

Numbers are on the rise. I'm wondering what makes for an unconfirmed shark attack. If a person has a huge chunk of meat ripped out of his arse, does anyone really suspect a sea bass?

• Brian Handwerk, "Shark Facts: Attack Stats, Record Swims, More," National Geographic News, June 13, 2005, www.news.nationalgeographic.com.

 F A C T: Collisions with motor vehicles cause over 90 per cent of deaths from bicycle-related injuries.

And it's not the people in the motor vehicles who die, in case you were wondering.

• "Bicycle Injury: A Nationwide Problem," Alaska Department of Transportation, August 2003, www.dot.alaska.gov.

 F A C T: In 2008, a seventeen-year-old boy was killed at Six Flags Over Georgia amusement park after being decapitated by a roller coaster. The teen and a friend had climbed over two well-marked six-foot security fences as a short-cut into the park when the victim was struck.

Six Flags' 'No pushing in line' policy is a bit more strict than most amusement parks.

• "Boy Decapitated by Rollercoaster at Six Flags Over Georgia," Atlanta Journal-Constitution, June 29, 2008, www.ajc.com.

 F A C T: A thirty-two-year-old woman fell from a roller coaster at Holiday World & Splashin' Safari theme park in Santa Claus, Indiana in 2003 and was killed. The equipment malfunctioned at the highest point of the roller coaster, when riders feel the most 'air time,' or zero-gravity feeling as a roller coaster train crests a hill. The victim fell from the last seat of the train car and plunged to her death.

You'd think nothing bad could happen in a town called Santa Claus. You'd be wrong.

• "Woman, 32, Killed in Fall from Roller Coaster at Holiday World," RideAccidents.com, May 31, 2003, www.rideaccidents.com.

F A C T: The U.S. has only 4 per cent of the world's population, but consumes 65 per cent of its supply of hard drugs.

Except when Amy Winehouse is in the country; then it jumps to 95 per cent.

• "Drugs: America's Problem with Illicit Drugs," Narconon, www.stopaddiction.com.

 F A C T: Regularly snorting cocaine can lead to nasal problems, such as nosebleeds, loss of sense of smell, hoarseness, problems with swallowing, and septum irritation which leads to a chronically inflamed, runny nose.

It can also rot your nose until it falls off your face. That's a nasal problem.

• "Cocaine," Psychology Today, www.psychologytoday.com.

 F A C T: Cocaine users who inject the drug intravenously may have allergic reactions to the drug or any of the additives commonly found in street cocaine, which can result in death in severe cases. Users who inject the drug also risk acquiring HIV infection/AIDS and Hepatitis C if they share needles and injection equipment.

Sharing needles shows a lack of judgment. People who buy illicit drugs from strangers and shoot them directly into their veins should know better.

• "Cocaine," Psychology Today, www.psychologytoday.com.

 F A C T: Potentially dangerous interactions can occur when taking cocaine and alcohol in any combination. Both drugs convert to cocaethylene in the body, which is more toxic and has a longer duration in the brain than either drug alone. The mixture creates the most common fatal two-drug combination.

I think more toxic and longer duration is the whole point.

• "Cocaine," Psychology Today, www.psychologytoday.com.

 F A C T: Smoking causes acute myeloid leukemia, as well as cancer in other areas of the body, including the bladder, mouth, larynx (voice box), cervix, kidneys, lungs, esophagus, pancreas, and stomach.

Bladder cancer sounds like fun.

• "Fact Sheet – Health Effects of Cigarette Smoking," Centres for Disease Control and Prevention, National Centre for Chronic Disease Prevention and Health Promotion, Office on Smoking and Health, January 2008, www.cdc.gov.

 F A C T: Smoking nearly doubles a person's risk of having a stroke.

And triples his risk of being asked, 'Can I scrounge a cigarette?'

• "Fact Sheet – Health Effects of Cigarette Smoking," Centres for Disease Control and Prevention, National Centre for Chronic Disease Prevention and Health Promotion, Office on Smoking and Health, January 2008, www.cdc.gov.

 F A C T: About 18 per cent of women aged fifteen to forty-four smoke cigarettes while pregnant.

You'd think that a fifteen-year-old pregnant girl would have better judgment.

• "The Health Consequences of Involuntary Exposure to Tobacco Smoke: A Report of the Surgeon General," U.S. Department of Health and Human Services, Centres for Disease Control and Prevention, National Centre for Chronic Disease Prevention and Health Promotion, Office on Smoking and Health, 2006, www.surgeongeneral.gov.

 F A C T: Smoking is more prevalent among women who live below the poverty level than women living at or above it.

Well, they've got do something while they're filling out lottery tickets.

• "The Health Consequences of Involuntary Exposure to Tobacco Smoke: A Report of the Surgeon General," U.S. Department of Health and Human Services, Centres for Disease Control and Prevention, National Centre for Chronic Disease Prevention and Health Promotion, Office on Smoking and Health, 2006, www.surgeongeneral.gov.

 F A C T: Exposure to passive smoke can produce immediate adverse effects on the cardiovascular system, interfering with the way the heart, blood, and vascular systems normally function, and increasing the risk of a heart attack.

Yes, but passive smokers get to smoke for free! Think of all the money they're saving.

• "The Health Consequences of Involuntary Exposure to Tobacco Smoke: A Report of the Surgeon General," U.S. Department of Health and Human Services, Centres for Disease Control and Prevention, National Centre for Chronic Disease Prevention and Health Promotion, Office on Smoking and Health, 2006, www.surgeongeneral.gov.

F A C T: Excessive alcohol use, either as heavy drinking or binge drinking, can result in increased health problems, like liver disease, psychological disorders, unintentional injuries, and more.

Death is another increased health problem caused by heavy drinking.

• "Alcohol-Attributable Deaths Report, Average for United States 2001–2005," Centres for Disease Control and Prevention, National Centre for Chronic Disease Prevention and Health Promotion, https://apps.nccd.cdc.gov.

F A C T: Heroin withdrawal symptoms include muscle and bone pain, restlessness, insomnia, vomiting, diarrhoea, cold flashes with goose bumps (hence the term, 'cold turkey'), and involuntary leg movements.

That's nine good reasons not to stop.

• "Research Report Series – Heroin Abuse and Addiction," National Institute on Drug Abuse, U.S. Department of Health and Human Services, July 22, 2008, www.nida.nih.gov.

F A C T: Withdrawal symptoms from heroin peak twenty-four to forty-eight hours after last use and usually subside within about a week, although some users endure them for many months.

The involuntary leg movements include kicking yourself repeatedly in the arse for ever trying the drug in the first place. But involuntarily.

• "Research Report Series – Heroin Abuse and Addiction," National Institute on Drug Abuse, U.S. Department of Health and Human Services, July 22, 2008, www.nida.nih.gov.

F A C T: Caffeine is more addictive than marijuana.

But you can drink coffee in your office without turning off the lights and putting on Dark Side Of The Moon.

• "The Most Addictive Drugs," Teen Drug Rehab Treatment Centres – Alcohol and Drug Rehabs for Young Adults – Addiction Treatment, www.drugrehabtreatment.com.

F A C T: In severe cases, caffeine overdose can result in death from convulsions or an irregular heartbeat.

Caffeine underdose – i.e., not getting your morning coffee – has similar results: anxiety, depression, convulsions. It can also result in a swift and severe death to anyone who pisses you off.

• "Quick Facts: Caffeine," CNN Food Central, www.cnn.com.
• David Zieve, Greg Juhn, and David R. Eltz, "Caffeine Overdose," Medline Plus, U.S. National Library of Medicine and the National Institutes of Health, January 23, 2008, www.nlm.nih.gov.

 F A C T: Heavy and chronic use of marijuana damages short-term memory and may impair the ability to form memories, recall events, and shift attention from one thing to another.

It can also lead to, uhh, it can lead to... wait... what?

• "Your Brain on Marijuana," Teen Drug Rehab Treatment Centres – Alcohol and Drug Rehabs for Young Adults – Addiction Treatment, www.drugrehabtreatment.com.

 F A C T: Swedish researchers have discovered a link between marijuana use and heightened risk of developing schizophrenia.

Sounds like the Swedes need to work on growing better weed.

• "Marijuana Myths and Facts: The Truth Behind 10 Popular Misconceptions," Office of National Drug Control Policy, www.whitehousedrugpolicy.gov.

 F A C T: Pseudoephedrine or ephedrine is the most common ingredient used in methamphetamine (crystal meth), also found in cold medicine. Other ingredients used are ether, paint thinner, Freon, acetone, drain cleaner, battery acid, and lithium.

Which, coincidentally, is nearly identical to the recipe for kebabs.

• Meth Awareness," U.S. Department Of Justice, www.usdoj.gov.

GET ME A DOCTOR!

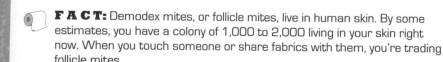

Bodies, bugs and bogs

FACT: Demodex mites, or follicle mites, live in human skin. By some estimates, you have a colony of 1,000 to 2,000 living in your skin right now. When you touch someone or share fabrics with them, you're trading follicle mites.

Unless you touch someone's heart, in which case you don't give them follicle mites, but a warm fuzzy feeling inside. It's a figure of speech, you see.

• Yezid Gutiérrez, Diagnostic Pathology of Parasitic Infections with Clinical Correlations, 2nd ed. (Oxford University Press, 2000).

FACT: Humans develop schistosomiasis after contact with water containing snails infected by human waste. Snail larvae infiltrate the body and grow into adult worms which are up to half an inch long. They live in the bloodstream and can cause inflammation, organ enlargement, intestinal bleeding, bladder cancer, and death.

I'll take death. Thanks.

• Coco Ballantyne, "Worms 'N Us: A Look at 8 Parasitic Worms That Live in Humans," Scientific American, February 5, 2009, www.sciam.com.

F A C T: Approximately half the world's population is infected with large roundworms, hookworms, or whipworms. A Columbia University parasitologist calls them the 'unholy trinity.'

I prefer to think of them as the intestinal worm version of the Marx brothers: Groucho (roundworm), Harpo (hookworm), and Chico (whipworm). The tapeworm, a less common intestinal parasite, is Zeppo, who didn't always appear with the other three.

• Coco Ballantyne, "Worms 'NUs: A Look at 8 Parasitic Worms That Live in Humans," Scientific American, February 5, 2009, www.sciam.com.

F A C T: Ascariasis is the most common worm related infection found in humans. Symptoms such as fever, shortness of breath, and wheezing result from roundworm larvae infesting the lungs. The larvae then migrate to the intestines, where they grow to resemble foot-long earthworms.

Once again, I will take death over a foot-long earthworm in my arse, thanks.

• Coco Ballantyne, "Worms 'NUs: A Look at 8 Parasitic Worms That Live in Humans," Scientific American, February 5, 2009, www.sciam.com.

F A C T: Ascariasis affects as many as 1.5 billion people worldwide, causing 60,000 deaths per year.

The ones who don't die always have bait at the ready if they want to go fishing.

• Coco Ballantyne, "Worms 'N Us: A Look at 8 Parasitic Worms That Live in Humans," Scientific American, February 5, 2009, www.sciam.com

F A C T: About 800 million people worldwide are infected with whipworm, which can cause diarrhoea, weight loss, and anemia. In severe instances rectal prolapse can occur, in which the walls of the rectum protrude from the anus.

You might know rectal prolapse by its colourful street name: arse tulip.

• Coco Ballantyne, "Worms 'NUs: A Look at 8 Parasitic Worms That Live in Humans," Scientific American, February 5, 2009, www.sciam.com.

FACT: Unlike most parasitic worms that inhabit the intestines, lymphatic filariae live in the body's lymph system, where they can cause swelling of the legs, arms, breasts, and, in men especially, the genitalia. More than 120 million people worldwide are infected, a third of them disfigured by the condition.

No man I know would object to enlarged genitalia.

• Coco Ballantyne, "Worms 'NUs: A Look at 8 Parasitic Worms That Live in Humans," Scientific American, February 5, 2009, www.sciam.com.

FACT: Every time your heart beats, it pumps a quarter of your blood to the head. Brain cells then process 20 per cent of the oxygen and food your blood contains. Conditions that disrupt circulation – such as heart disease, diabetes, and stroke – appear to increase the chances of developing dementia and Alzheimer's disease.

It's like getting free sprinkles on your sundae. Except it's a shit sundae, and the sprinkles are maggots.

• "Risk Factors," Alzheimer's Association, www.alz.org.

FACT: According to a researcher, you can stay healthy and combat allergy symptoms by rinsing the nose with salt water.

I've heard that a colonic is also good for you, but I won't be doing that, either.

• "Twenty-five Things You Probably Didn't Know About Your Body and Health," MSN Health, www.health.msn.com.

FACT: Traumatic brain injury (TBI) is a serious health problem for people aged seventy-five and older, as they have the highest rates of TBIs and tend to recover more slowly or die from their injuries. TBI symptoms are subtle, and may not even appear until days or even weeks after the injury occurs.

The rate of TBI in Britian is still TBC. Consider it TBA until further notice.

• "Help Seniors Live Better, Longer: Prevent Brain Injury," Centres for Disease Control and Prevention, www.cdc.gov.

F A C T: Blowing your nose when you have a cold might feel good, but it can actually worsen your condition. Blowing generates enormous pressure and propels mucus into the sinuses, spreading viruses or bacteria and potentially causing further infection.

What's the alternative? Just letting the snot run down your face?

• Ana had O'Connor, "The Claim: Never Blow Your Nose When You Have a Cold," New York Times, February 9, 2009, www.nytimes.com.

F A C T: Bacteria can grow and divide every twenty minutes, turning one bacterial cell into 16 million in just eight hours.

Bacteria sound a lot like trivia facts.

• Michael Stringer and C.Dennis, Chilled Foods: A Comprehensive Guide, 2nd ed. (Woodhead Publishing, 2000).

F A C T: Belly button fluff is made up of clothing fibres, dead skin, and more. You should keep your navel clean and dry to prevent infection from candida, a type of fungus.

That's why I call it navel jam. 'Fluff' doesn't fully capture the variety and complexity of the recipe.

• Perry Garfinkel, The Male Body: An Owner's Manual: The Ultimate Head-to-Toe Guide to Staying Healthy and Fit for Life (Rodale, 1996).

F A C T: Erectile dysfunction (ED) is a man's inability to keep an erection long enough to perform sexual intercourse. As many as 80 per cent of men seventy-five and older have erectile dysfunction, but the problem can occur at any age. Causes include lung, liver, heart, or kidney disease; endocrine system disorders such as diabetes; side effects of antidepressants and other medications; substance or alcohol abuse; and anxiety and depression.

They should call premature ejaculation 'projectile dysfunction (PD),' just for the sake of consistency.

• "Erectile Dysfunction," Mayo Clinic, www.mayoclinic.com.

FACT: High heels are blamed by orthopedists for chronic back problems and postural difficulties. Wearing high-heel shoes regularly causes the tendon in the leg to shrink, making it painful to wear flat shoes. Some even blame high heels for problems with the internal organs in the abdomen, since the distortion of posture pushes the pelvic region out of normal alignment.

But they're so comfortable.

• Robin Tolmach Lakoff and Raquel L. Scherr, Face Value, the Politics of Beauty: The Politics of Beauty (Routledge, 1984).

FACT: A sneeze expels germ-filled droplets to distances of up to thirty feet. The water content of the droplets evaporates quickly, but thousands of virus cells remain suspended in the air and can infect others.

This is why I like to sneeze in people's hair. No germs are suspended in the air, plus it's fun to watch the reactions, especially from strangers.

• Jana Balaram, Preventive and Social Medicine (B. JainPublishers, 2002).

FACT: Never share mascara, as this is the most common way that people pass on eye infections like conjunctivitis (pinkeye), which is highly contagious.

I hope The Cure's Robert Smith is reading this.

• Stephen W. Moore, H. Winter Griffith, and Kenneth Yoder, Complete Guide To Symptoms, Illness & Surgery (Perigee, 2006).

FACT: Nearly 70 per cent of poisoning deaths in 2004 were ruled accidental. Another 19 per cent were suicides, while the rest were categorised as manslaughter or undetermined.

What some call accidental is really just Darwinism at work – cleaning out the gene pool and what not.

• "Question of the Month:" What is the second leading cause of death by injury in the United States?" The Nation's Health, May 2008, www.apha.org.

FACT: A study published in March 2009 reported overweight eighteen-year-old men were as likely to die by sixty as occasional smokers. Obese young men, much like heavy smokers, doubled the risk of dying early.

So you have a choice, young fatties: donuts or cigarettes. It's a tough one, I know. Good luck.

• Roni Caryn Rabin, "Obese Teens as Likely as Smokers to Die Early, Study Finds," New York Times, March 3, 2009. www.nytimes.com.

 FACT: In humans with celiac disease, the body's immune system damages the lining of the small intestine when it processes gluten, hindering the body's ability to absorb nutrients from food and causes digestive problems. Untreated celiac disease can be life-threatening.

Other names for celiac disease are celiac sprue and gluten intolerance, but I like to call it 'pootin' gluten.'

• "What I Need to Know about Celiac Disease," National Digestive Diseases Information Clearinghouse, National Institute of Diabetes and Digestive and Kidney Diseases, National Institutes of Health, www.digestive.niddk.nih.gov.
• "Celiac Disease Facts," University of Maryland Centre for Celiac Research, www.umm.edu.

 FACT: Eating disorders such as anorexia and bulimia can cause low blood pressure, diabetes, heart and kidney problems, brain damage and death.

Other than that, they're harmless.

• "Eating Disorders," Medline Plus, National Institutes of Health, Department of Health & Human Services, February 27, 2009, www.nlm.nih.gov.

 FACT: Conditions that affect less than 200,000 people nationwide are characterized as orphan diseases. These include Lou Gehrig's disease, cystic fibrosis, Tourette's syndrome, and lesser-known conditions such as Job syndrome, Hamburger disease, and gigantism.

Huh, I always thought orphan diseases were things like lice and rickets.

• Carol Rados, "Orphan Products: Hope for People With Rare Diseases," FDA Consumer Magazine, November–December 2003, www.fda.gov.

F A C T: The medical condition known as heart failure does not mean that your heart has arrested or is about to stop working, but that the organ isn't pumping enough blood through the body.

Either way, it ain't great.

• "Heart Failure," Medline Plus, National Institutes of Health, Department of Health & Human Services, www.nlm.nih.gov.

F A C T: Humans can grow horns. Called cutaneous horns, they grow when the skin surface thickens, typically in response to disease.

I'm pretty sure my old boss had some but not because she was diseased – because she was the Devil.

• Diane Mapes, "These Aren't Devil's Horns, They're Real," The Body Odd, MSNBC.com, www.bodyodd.msnbc.msn.com.

F A C T: A ninety-two-year-old Chinese woman recently gave birth to a sixty-year-old baby.

No baby wants to come out of the womb, but some are a little more stubborn than others. Oh, and by the way – ouch.

• Diane Mapes, "The Curious Case Of The Stone Baby," The Body Odd, MSNBC.com, www.bodyodd.msnbc.msn.com.

F A C T: A sixty-year-old British woman cannot recognise voices, even those of family members. She can't comprehend who is talking to her unless she can see the speaking person's face. Even if her child calls on the telephone, it is as if she is hearing that voice for the first time. The only exception is Sean Connery's voice.

But only when he says, 'Suck it, Trebek.'

• Brian Alexander, "Unable To Recognise Voices, Unless It's Sean Connery," The Body Odd, MSNBC. com, www.bodyodd.msnbc.msn.com.

F A C T: Researchers in Germany have discovered that, if exposed to an unpleasant smell, sleepers will have bad dreams. When exposed to pleasant smells of roses, the opposite occurred and their dreams were subsequently positive.

That is, if you consider dreaming that you're a gardener positive.

• Mark Leyner and Billy Goldberg, "Bad Smells Can Give You Nightmares," The Body Odd, MSNBC. com, www.bodyodd.msnbc.msn.com.

 FACT: If you sneeze hard enough, you can fracture a rib. But try to suppress a sneeze and you might rupture a blood vessel in your head or neck and drop dead.

If you try to suppress a fart and a sneeze at the same time, you could blow your head off like a champagne cork.

• Cameron Tuttle, The Paranoid's Pocket Guide (Chronicle Books, 1997).

 FACT: While pubic lice primarily infect pubic hair, they can also be found in thigh, chest, and facial hair, including eyelashes.

How pubic lice might end up on one's face I will leave to you to deduce.

• James G.H. Dinulos, MD, "Lice," Merck Manuals Online Medical Library, September 2008, www.merck.com.

 FACT: The human stomach must produce a new lining every day to protect itself from its own acid.

Which somehow reminds me of Groucho Marx's quote, 'I don't care to belong to any club that would have me as a member.'

• Matthew Fox, The A.W.E .Project: Reinventing Education, Reinventing the Human (WoodLake Publishing, 2006

 FACT: The acid in your stomach is so powerful that it can dissolve a razor blade in less than a week.

You should still be careful when eating them, though.

• Matthew Fox, The A.W.E. Project: Reinventing Education, Reinventing the Human (WoodLake Publishing, 2006).

 FACT: If a boy is born without testosterone, his genitalia will mimic that of a female: the scrotum forms labia majora – the outer lips of a vagina – and the penis becomes a sort of clitoris.

That's the guy you don't want to tell to go fuck himself, because he might try.

• Ruth K. Westheimer, Sex for Dummies, 3rd ed. (For Dummies, 2006).

 F A C T: The skin is the largest organ in the human body, covering about twenty square feet in an adult male. It also constantly regenerates; a person sheds around 40lbs of skin in his lifetime.

Some people can shed it all at once by just shaking their dandruff-ridden heads.

• Robert Dolezal, Reader's Digest Book of Facts (Readers Digest, 1987).
• Mitchell Symons, That Book:. . . of Perfectly Useless Information (Harper Collins, 2004).

 F A C T: We grow in our sleep, and wake up every morning about eight millimetres taller than the night before. However, we return to our former height as gravity compresses our cartilage discs back into place throughout the next day.

It's like 'morning wood' for the entire body.

• Robert Dolezal, Reader's Digest Book of Facts (Readers Digest, 1987).

 F A C T: The pressure exerted by a pumping human heart can squirt blood thirty feet.

Research is limited, though, so if you ever lose a limb unexpectedly, grab a tape measure and see how far your blood squirts before you pass out and die. Don't forget to write it down, too.

• Mitchell Symons, That Book:. . . of Perfectly Useless Information (Harper Collins, 2004).

 F A C T: You can find 20 million microscopic animals living on a square inch of human skin.

Skin sounds like Tokyo.

• Mitchell Symons, That Book: . . . of Perfectly Useless Information (Harper Collins, 2004).

FACT: The average human body radiates enough heat in thirty minutes to boil two pints of water.

But only if you're not looking. A watched body won't boil.

• Robert Dolezal, Reader's Digest Book of Facts (Readers Digest, 1987).

FACT: Though female ovaries generate almost half a million eggs, only about 400 of them will ever get the chance to be fertilized.

It's like being called for jury service, except the eggs probably don't sit there whispering to themselves, 'Please don't pick me, please don't pick me.'

• Robert Dolezal, Reader's Digest Book of Facts (Readers Digest, 1987).

FACT: Human saliva helps keep the mouth's pH balance slightly alkaline. If it didn't, the mouth would create an acidic environment that would rot away your teeth.

If the acid is that strong, you won't need teeth.

• Kathleen McGowan, "The Biology of . . . Saliva," Discover, October 2005, www.discovermagazine.com.

FACT: There are over 700 species of bacteria that thrive in the thirty-three square inches of the average mouth, making it the most unsanitary part of your entire body.

Surely the rectum runs a close second?

• "Grossology Gross Facts," Denver Museum of Natural Science, www.dmns.org.

FACT: By the time you're an adult, you're likely to have about 5 million hairs growing out of your skin – the same number as a gorilla.

Or Robin Williams.

• "Human Hair," Discovery Channel, http://.yucky.discovery.com.

F A C T: Male testicles create 10 million new sperm cells every day, enough to repopulate the planet in just six months.

Some men try, too.

• Robert Dolezal, Reader's Digest Book of Facts (Readers Digest, 1987).

F A C T: Being 'scared to death' can happen. The body's protective mechanism – the fight-or-flight response – pumps adrenaline into the blood, causing the nervous system to increase blood flow to muscles, dilate the pupils and, in some cases, evacuate the bowels. But adrenaline is toxic in large amounts and can cause death if it floods the heart unchecked.

So being 'scared shitless' isn't just hyperbole, either.

• Coco Ballantyne, "Can a person be scared to death?" Scientific American, January 30, 2009, www.sciam.com.

F A C T: Strong positive or negative emotions – ecstasy, grief, excitement – can lead to sudden cardiac death via ventricular fibrillation (irregular heartbeat), as in the case of people who have died during sexual intercourse or when frightened.

Or when frightened during sexual intercourse, which happens more often than you might think. At least it does to me.

• Coco Ballantyne, "Can a person be scared to death?" Scientific American, January 30, 2009, www.sciam.com

F A C T: Some people are born with extra nipples (polythelia) or even extra breasts (polymastia). Extra or 'accessory' breasts are most commonly found in the armpits, but can develop anywhere along mammary ridges, which extend from the armpits to the upper thighs.

And, by the way, we still don't know why men have a mammary ridge, just that they do.

• Leonard V. Crowley, An Introduction to Human Disease: Pathology and Pathophysiology Correlations, 7th ed. (Jones & Bartlett, 2006).
• Susan Van Houten, "Accessory nipples (polythelia) and breast tissue (polymastia),"University Health Systems Of Eastern Carolina, March 21, 2003, www.uhseast.com.

F A C T: Breast cancer isn't just a women's disease. Men can also get it, although less frequently – about one man for every 100 women. Also, unlike women, men typically only get the disease after the age of fifty.

Sounds like a good excuse to go into the mobile mammography bus and scope out some bare boobs.

• Gerard M. Doherty and Lawrence W. Way, Current Surgical Diagnosis & Treatment, 12th ed. [McGraw-Hill, 2005].

F A C T: Humans shed about 1.5 million skin flakes every hour. Bath sponges and wash cloths can be filled with these flakes and their accompanying staphy lococcus aureus, a common skin bacteria that can cause infection if it ends up in the wrong part of the body.

In other words, don't wash your crack with someone else's loofa unless you want to spend the next six months scratching it.

• Philip M. Tierno, The Secret Life of Germs: What They Are, Why We Need Them, and How We Can Protect Ourselves against Them [Simon & Schuster, 2004].

F A C T: Only 10 per cent of the cells in our bodies are actually human. The rest are the 90 trillion bacteria that live on or in us, covering our bodies from head to toe.

Only 5 per cent of the cells in Christopher Walken's body are actually human. The rest are from an alien world.

• Rose George, The Big Necessity: The Unmentionable World of Human Waste and Why It Matters [St. Martin's Press, 2008].
• Garry Hamilton, "Insider Trading," New Scientist, June 26, 1999, www.newscientist.com.

F A C T: Sleep disturbs normal metabolism, which contributes to obesity, diabetes, and cardiovascular disease. People who averaged just five hours of sleep a night also showed a higher level of ghrelin, a hormone released by the stomach to signal hunger.

People who average just five hours of sleep a night also show a higher level of ghrouch, a hormone that makes you want to kick someone's arse when they say, 'You look tired.'

• Rick Nauert, PhD, "Childhood Obesity from Lack of Sleep?" PsychCentral, October 24, 2006,http://psychcentral.com.

FACT: All humans exist for half an hour as a single cell at conception.

Some of us stay that way.

• Truman Hedding, "Nineteen Things You Didn't Know About The Human Body," www.trumanhedding.com.

FACT: Continuous farting for six years and nine months would create energy equal to that of an atomic bomb.

I need to hook my child up with the Defense Department.

• Mitchell Symons, That Book:. . . of Perfectly Useless Information (Harper Collins, 2004).

FACT: Your body produces enough saliva during your lifetime to fill two swimming pools.

Luckily, most swimming pools are already filled with saliva, so yours isn't needed.

• Mary M. Bauer, The Truth About You: Things You Don't Know You Know (Vander Wyk &Burnham, 2006).

FACT: The human liver performs no fewer than 500 different functions. If a portion of it were removed, the liver would continue to work and would rapidly grow back to its normal size.

Well, depending on the size of the portion. Don't go lopping off huge chunks of your liver to give away, okay?

• Mary M. Bauer, The Truth About You: Things You Don't Know You Know (Vander Wyk &Burnham, 2006).

FACT: Seventy per cent of people admit to picking their nose; 30 per cent of those confess to eating what they picked.

100 per cent of people admit to vomiting when they read that.

• "Grossology Gross Facts," Denver Museum of Natural Science,www.dmns.org

F A C T: Believe it or not, fresh urine is cleaner than saliva or your facial skin. Healthy urine is sterile and contains little or no bacteria when it leaves your body.

Being cleaner than spit isn't really a bragging point.

• "Grossology Gross Facts," Denver Museum of Natural Science, www.dmns.org.
• "Bacteria in Urine, No Symptoms," University Of Michigan Health System, www.med.umich.edu.

 F A C T: Research suggests that marital discord makes wounds heal more slowly. A recent study showed that couples with consistently hostile behaviours healed at a 40 per cent slower rate than low hostility couples.

Which means you're gonna have that shoemark on your forehead for a while.

• J.K. Kiecolt-Glase, "Hostile Marital Interactions, Proinflammatory Cytokine Production, and Wound Healing," Archives of General Psychiatry, December2005, http://.archpsyc.ama-assn.org.

 F A C T: Babies are born without kneecaps – sort of. They have cartilage in their kneecaps which does not ossify into bone until 3–5 years of age.

This explains why infants are notorious gamblers. They don't have to worry about having their kneecaps broken if they don't pay their bookies.

• Noel Botham, The Ultimate Book of Useless Information: A Few Thousand More Things You Might Need to Know (But Probably Don't) (Perigee, 2007).
• Tom Scheve, "Do Babies Have Kneecaps?" HowStuffWorks.com, www.health.howstuffworks.com.

 F A C T: Your nose can remember 50,000 different scents.

So, unlike a dog, once you sniff someone's crotch, you'll remember the smell and won't have to sniff them again later. That's a good thing, because sticking your nose in someone's crotch is a good way to get thrown out of a bar, trust me.

• "Sixteen Unusual Facts About The Human Body," HowStuffWorks.com, www.health. howstuffworks.com.

FACT: About 1 in 2,000 babies are born with teeth. If the teeth are membranous, they will be reabsorbed into the body. If fixed firmly, don't remove them, or no other teeth will reappear in their place until the permanent teeth start to come in at age six or seven.

It's easy to spot a baby with teeth. He's the one drinking from a bottle instead of breast feeding.

• Adele Pillitteri. Maternal &Child Health Nursing: Care of the Childbearing & Childrearing Family, 5th ed. (Lippincott Williams& Wilkins, 2006).

FACT: Copremesis, or faecal vomiting, is not a myth: a bowel obstruction can cause faeces to be drawn into the stomach from the intestine by spasmodic contractions of the gastric muscles, which the stomach then attempts to expel through vomiting.

That explains some people's breath.

• "Faecal Vomiting," Dorland's Medical Dictionary, www.mercksource.com.
• "Faecal Vomiting," Medical Dictionary, www.medicaldictionary.com.
• "Faecal Vomiting," Poop Report,www.poopreport.com.

FACT: Smegma is a white, foul-smelling, cheeselike secretion sometimes found under the foreskin in males and around the clitoris in females. Smegma is produced by body oils and the bacteria that feed on them. Some studies have suggested a link between smegma and penile and cervical cancer.

You had me at 'cheese-like.'

• "What is smegma?" NetDoctorUK, www.netdoctor.co.uk.
• "Teen Talk: Smegma," Planned Parenthood, www.teenwire.com.
• "What are the risk factors for penile cancer?" Cancer.org, www.cancer.org.

FACT: A person can live without eating for weeks, but will only survive eleven days without sleep.

People around those who haven't slept, however, will only survive a day or two.

• "Sixteen Unusual Facts About The Human Body," How Stuff Works, www.health.howstuffworks.com.

F A C T: The human brain stops growing at the age of eighteen. Probably because most eighteen-year-olds know everything by then.

If you don't believe me, ask them.

• Facts Library, FactLib.com, www.factlib.com.

F A C T: The germs on your fingers double after using the toilet, but almost 50 per cent of men and 25 per cent of women do not wash their hands after going to the loo.

That's why they call bowls of sweets in pubs and restaurants 'faecal mints.'

• Katy Holland and Sarah Jarvis, Children's Health for Dummies (For Dummies, 2006).

F A C T: Simply washing your hands with soap and water after going to the toilet reduces the spread of diarrhoeal diseases by almost half.

The simple act of diarrhoea is enough to convince me to wash my hands with soap.

• "Poo Facts," Poo Productions Advocacy Group, www.pooproductions.org.

F A C T: Some intestinal viruses can remain in the air after you defecate and flush the toilet, and can cause infection if inhaled or swallowed.

Why are you inhaling anyway? You like that smell? I hold my breath until I can get the hell out of there.

• J. Barker and M.V. Jones, "The Potential Spread of Infection Caused by Aerosol Contamination of Surfaces after Flushing a Domestic Toilet," Department of Pharmaceutical and Biological Sciences, School of Life and Health Sciences, Aston University, www.ncbi.nlm.nih.gov.

F A C T: In a humid environment like a bathroom, a single bacterial cell can multiply into 1 billion cells overnight.

I imagine that all that floating, flying faeces doesn't help either.

• Philip M. Tierno, The Secret Life of Germs: What They Are, Why We Need Them, and Howe Can Protect Ourselves Against Them (Simon & Schuster, 2004), 92.

FACT: Forty per cent of the world's population have no toilet, and must use the loo in any public place that they can find: bushes, roadsides, alleys, etc.

Roadsides sound especially fun. 'Dad, can I borrow the car? I wanna go out and take a shit.'

• Rose George, The Big Necessity: The Unmentionable World of Human Waste and Why It Matters (St. Martin's Press, 2008).

FACT: Faeces in the water supply cause 10 per cent of the world's communicable diseases.

On a moonless night, a well can easily be mistaken for a latrine.

• Rose George, The Big Necessity: The Unmentionable World of Human Waste and Why It Matters (St. Martin's Press, 2008).

FACT: People often fart shortly after they die.

Is this what they mean by a 'death rattle'?

• "Facts On Farts," SmellyPoop.com, www.smellypoop.com.

FACT: Safe disposal of children's faeces can reduce childhood diarrhoea by as much as 40 per cent.

A few years ago I took my dogs for a walk. One of them went off the trail to sniff around and started wallowing in something on the ground. When the dog returned, he stank of what I assumed to be deer faeces. We hiked on and the path curved around by the spot where my dog had wallowed, so I glanced over... and saw a big pile of used toilet paper. That was not safe disposal of faeces.
• "Poo Facts," Poo Productions Advocacy Group, www.pooproductions.org.

FACT: The most germ-laden place on your toilet isn't the seat or even the bowl: it's the handle.

The solution: don't flush. Let the next person worry about it.

• "The Truth about the Toilet," Clorox.com, www.clorox.com.

FACT: Some major world cities remain disturbingly behind the times when it comes to sanitation. Milan, Italy, one of the fashion centres of the world, continued to dump raw, dangerous sewage into the Lambro River until the city built its first treatment plant in 2005, spurred by the threat of a $15-million-a-day fine from the European Union.

And you thought that Venice smelled bad.

• Rose George, The Big Necessity: The Unmentionable World of Human Waste and Why It Matters (St. Martin's Press, 2008).

F A C T: When you wee, a small amount of urine enters your mouth through the saliva glands.

Which I suppose is better than urine entering your mouth any other way.

• Greta Garbage, That's Disgusting: An Adult Guide to What's Gross, Tasteless, Rude, Crude, and Lewd (Ten Speed Press, 1999).

F A C T: Urine with a sweet odour can indicate that blood sugar is being excreted, a warning sign for diabetes. The smell is also caused by starvation and ketonuria, a result of excessive dieting.

I don't think that starving people are too concerned about the smell of their wee.

• Sally Wadyka, "What Your Urine is Telling You About Your Health," MSN Health & Fitness, www.health.msn.com.

F A C T: If you see blood in your urine, consult your doctor right away. It is most likely the sign of a urinary tract infection, but can also indicate bladder cancer.

Yes, see a doctor right away – after you regain consciousness, that is.

• Sally Wadyka, "What Your Urine is Telling You About Your Health," MSN Health & Fitness, www.health.msn.com.

F A C T: Holding in urine too long puts you at risk of death from hyponatremia, also called 'water intoxication,' the result of consuming more water than your body can regulate. In 2007, a twenty-eight-year-old woman died of hyponatremia during a 'Hold Your Wee for a Wii' contest sponsored by a local radio station in Sacramento, California.

Well, her New Year's resolution was to drink more water.

• Tom Zeller Jr., "Too High a Price for a Wii," The Lede – New Yok Times, January 15, 2007,
http://thelede.blogs.nytimes.com.

 F A C T: Red urine can indicate diabetic nephropathy, papillary renal cell carcinoma, or aloe poisoning. It can also be a sign that you ate too much beetroot, or a side effect of taking certain prescription drugs.

If you eat enough beetroot to turn your pee red, you might be a rabbit. Consult your local veterinarian.

• "Causes of Red urine," Wrong-Diagnosis.com, March 17, 2009, www.wrongdiagnosis.com.
• Ruth Woodrow, Essentials of Pharmacology for Health Occupations, 4th ed. (Cengageb Learning, 2001), 247.
• Joseph T. DiPiro and others, Pharmacotherapy: A Pathophysiologic Approach, 7th ed. (McGraw-Hill Professional, 2008), 84.

 F A C T: Black urine can be a sign that you have alkaptonuria, a rare hereditary condition that causes pee to turn pitch black upon exposure to air. Black urine disease can cause arthritis, and can inhibit cardiac, pulmonary, and renal function.

Black urine can also inhibit your 'not-screaming-like-a-schoolgirl' function.

• J. C. Segen, The Dictionary of Modern Medicine (Taylor & Francis, 1992).

 F A C T: Green urine can result from infections caused by Pseudomonas aeruginosa, a bacteria found in soil and water. It can be fatal if it occurs in the lungs, urinary tract, or kidneys.

Exceptions: Kermit The Frog, The Incredible Hulk, leprechauns.

• Samer Qarah, "Pseudomonas aeruginosa Infections," WrongDiagnosis.com,
www.wrongdiagnosis.com.
• J. C. Segen, The Dictionary of Modern Medicine (Taylor &Francis, 1992).

 F A C T: A gram of faeces contains up to a million bacteria, ten times as many viruses, 100 worm eggs, and 1,000 parasitic cysts.

And sweetcorn.

• Rose George, The Big Necessity: The Unmentionable World of Human Waste and Why It Matters (St. Martin's Press, 2008).

 F A C T: The average healthy adult expels between 100g and 200g of faeces a day.

That sounds low. Did they include vegans? How about James Corden?

• The Merck Manuals Online Medical Library, Merck & Co., www.merck.com.

 F A C T: Some experts estimate that people who live without adequate sanitation inadvertently consume ten grams of faecal matter every day, potentially leading to infection, serious illness, and death.

So don't bother telling them to eat shit – they already do.

• Rose George, The Big Necessity: The Unmentionable World of Human Waste and Why It Matters (St. Martin's Press, 2008).

 F A C T: Thin stools can be an indicator of colon cancer or its precursor, polyps in the colon.

Or they can simply mean that you are a small dog, like a Chihuahua or a Sausage Dog.

• Sally Wadyka, "What Your Bowel Movements Are Telling You About Your Health," MSN Health & Fitness, www.health.msn.com.

 F A C T: If your stool is pale or greyish, you could have problems somewhere in your digestive tract, such as a blockage in the liver or a pancreatic disorder.

Or maybe your stool just needs a little sun. Try shitting on the beach for a week or two and see if that helps.

• Sally Wadyka, "What Your Bowel Movements Are Telling You About Your Health," MSN Health & Fitness, www.health.msn.com.

 F A C T: During pregnancy, a woman can develop a fistula, or a hole in the vaginal wall that allows urine to stream out constantly. In the olden days, women with fistulas frequently became outcasts from their families and communities because of their odour.

My wife develops a fistula with her hand whenever I talk about old girlfriends.

• Denise Grady, "After a Devastating Birth Injury, Hope," New York Times, February 23, 2009, www.nytimes.com.

 F A C T: A rectovaginal fistula is an abnormal connection between the rectum and the vagina that can lead to passing gas or stool through the vagina. The injury can be caused by childbirth, cancer, a complication from surgery, or an inflammatory bowel condition such as Crohn's disease.

Yes, passing stool through your vag is slightly abnormal.

• Mayo Clinic staff, "Rectovaginal Fistula," May 30, 2008, www.mayoclinic.com.

 F A C T: Steatorrhea is the presence of excess quantities of fat in stools, and is frequently a sign of a malabsorption syndrome such as celiac disease, cystic fibrosis, and chronic pancreatitis.

The first sign of steatorrhea? Floaters.

• Richard Ravel, Clinical Laboratory Medicine: Clinical Application of Laboratory Data, 6th ed. (Elsevier Health Sciences, 1994).

 F A C T: Faecal transplant is becoming an increasingly popular option in the treatment of severe bacterial infections such as the Superbug (Clostridium difficile), which is resistant to many antibiotics. The transplant calls for the use of disease-free faeces from a patient's close relative, whose bacteria somehow defeat the infection.

'Um, hi, Dad, how's it going? This is a little awkward, but I have a favour to ask...'

• Rose George, The Big Necessity: The Unmentionable World of Human Waste and Why It Matters (St. Martin's Press, 2008).

 F A C T: Most people produce one to four pints of gas and pass it approximately fourteen times daily.

Keep in mind that fourteen is an average. Some people fart more often,

cutting a steady stream of smaller 'fartettes' throughout the day, while others dispatch their gas with fewer but beefier blasts.

• "Gas in the Digestive Tract," National Digestive Diseases Information Clearing house, National Institute of Diabetes and Digestive and Kidney Diseases, National Institutes of Health, January 2008, www.digestive.niddk.nih.gov.

 FACT: The foul odour of flatulence comes from intestinal bacteria as it releases gases that contain sulfur and, in some cases, methane, one of the greenhouse gases responsible for global warming.

Please be aware of not only your carbon footprint, but your carbon arse-print.

• "Gas in the Digestive Tract," National Digestive Diseases Information Clearinghouse, National Institute of Diabetes and Digestive and Kidney Diseases, National Institutes of Health, January 2008, www.digestive.niddk.nih.gov.

 FACT: Adolf Hitler suffered from chronic flatulence, for which he took anti-gas pills containing a mixture of belladonna and strychnine, both known poisons. One theory blames these and other 'pernicious medications' prescribed for Hitler by a 'diabolical quack' doctor for changes in his personality and temperament in the early 1940s.

Who says the universe has no sense of humour?

• Robert G. L. Waite, The Psychopathic God: Adolf Hitler (Da Capo Press, 1993).
• Greta Garbage, That's Disgusting: An Adult Guide to What's Gross, Tasteless, Rude, Crude, and Lewd (Ten Speed Press,1999).

 FACT: Urolagnia – also known as 'water sports' or 'golden showers' – is a sexual fetish in which partners derive pleasure from being urinated on, urinating on others, or drinking urine. Psychologists often classify the practise as a form of sexual sadomasochism. Always discuss urolagnia with your partner before attempting it, as some people get pissed off when pissed on.

• D. Richard Laws and William T. O'Donohue, Sexual Deviance: Theory, Assessment, and Treatment, 2nd ed. (Guilford Press, 2008).

F A C T: Another waste-based fetish, coprophilia, focuses on defecation for sexual satisfaction, and can include eliminating on one's partner, and playing with or consuming faecal matter, which can have serious health risks.

Please come back when you've finished puking. There are a lot more great facts in the book.

• D. Richard Laws and William T. O'Donohue, Sexual Deviance: Theory, Assessment, and Treatment, 2nd ed. (Guilford Press, 2008).

F A C T: The average human will spend three years on the toilet during his lifetime.

Lifetime? That's only about four visits for my old man.

• David Boyle and Anita Roddick, Numbers (Anita Roddick Books, 2004).

F A C T: Omorashi is a fetish subculture in Japan dedicated to arousal from the feeling of having a full bladder. Omorashi porn videos commonly feature schoolgirls, female professionals, and other women attempting to appear dignified before succumbing to the urge to wet themselves.

Really, who isn't turned on by incontinence? No wonder nonagenarians have so much sex.

• "Top 10 Bizarre Fetishes," Listverse, September 24, 2007, www.listverse.com.

F A C T: In March 2009, a New York restaurant owner was arrested for unlawful surveillance after a customer noticed a video camera in the ladies' toilet. The camera, connected to the man's office computer so he could observe females using the loo, was attached to the ceiling with sellotape. It had only been installed for a day before being spotted.

It took them a whole day to spot it?

• Newsday, www.newsday.com.

F A C T: A recent report from the National Academy of Sciences, Institute of Medicine, estimates that hospitals make preventable medical errors that kill as many as 98,000 people each year – more than cancer, AIDS, and road accidents.

And not nearly as fun.

• Tamar Nordenberg, "Make No Mistake: Medical Errors Can Be Deadly Serious," FDA Consumer, U.S. Food and Drug Administration, September–October 2000, www.fda.gov.

 F A C T: Patients who endure errors in treatment while in hospital care typically face a one in four chance of death from the mistake.

Which means that the staff who make the mistakes face a three in four chance of getting their arses kicked.

• Tamar Nordenberg, "Make No Mistake: Medical Errors Can Be Deadly Serious," FDA Consumer, U.S. Food and Drug Administration, September–October 2000, www.fda.gov.

 F A C T: In 2007, a New York fertility doctor made headlines after accidentally using the wrong man's sperm to inseminate a woman's eggs. The Hispanic woman and her white husband realised the mistake upon giving birth to an African-American baby. Subsequent DNA tests confirmed that the baby was indeed another man's.

Thank goodness they got those DNA tests. They might never have known otherwise.

• Todd Venezia, "Black Baby Is Born to White Pair," New York Post, March 22, 2007.
• Naomi Cahn, Test Tube Families: Why the Fertility Market Needs Legal Regulation (NYU Press, 2009), 68.

 F A C T: In 2006, surgeons at a Los Angeles hospital removed the healthy right testicle of a forty seven-year-old man by mistake. There were several botched steps leading to the surgery which resulted in the error, including a mistake on the consent form and forgetting to mark the surgical site before the procedure.

That's just nuts.

• Julia Hallisy, The Empowered Patient: Hundreds of Life-Saving Facts, Action Steps and Strategies You Need to Know (The Empowered Patient, 2007).
• "SoCal Vet Claims Wrong Testicle Removed In Surgery," CBS5.com, April 5, 2007, www.cbs5.com.

F A C T : A surgeon removed the incorrect leg of a fifty-two-year-old patient by mistake during amputation in 1995. The team realised their error mid procedure, but too late in the process to save the leg.

Wanna get away?

• "Florida Hospital Surgeons Mistakenly Amputate Wrong Leg of Patient," Jet, March 20, 1995, www.findarticles.com.
• Robert M. Wachter, Understanding Patient Safety (McGraw-Hill Professional, 2007),

F A C T : In June 2000, a man was admitted to the University of Washington Medical Centre in Seattle to have a tumor removed. Doctors removed the growth, but left a 13 inch retractor in the patient's abdomen when they sewed him up – the fifth documented case of University of Washington surgeons leaving a medical instrument inside a patient after surgery.

Free parting gift for all surgery patients!

• Carol Smith, "Surgical Tools Left in Five Patients," Seattle Post-Intelligencer, www.seattlepi.nwsource.com.

F A C T : A minister was admitted to a hospital in West Virginia in 2006 for exploratory abdominal surgery to diagnose the cause of pain. An anesthesiologist gave him drugs to prevent his muscles from twitching during surgery, but not general anesthesia until after the first incision. The patient felt excruciating pain but was unable to move or communicate.

I bet that he communicated once the anesthesia wore off.

• Associated Press, "Family Sues after Man Gets Wide-Awake Surgery," MSNBC.com, www.msnbc.msn.com.

F A C T : In 2007, actor Dennis Quaid's newborn twins nearly died after receiving an overdose of a blood thinning drug, Heparin, at a Los Angeles hospital. Three premature babies were killed in 2006 due to a similar mistake, where nurses administered Heparin for adults instead of Hep-lock for children. The medications were stocked in the wrong cabinet.

I bet no one at the hospital got his autograph after that.

• Dan Childs, "Medical Errors, Past and Present," November 27, 2007, ABC News, www.abcnews.com.

FACT: The drug Mirapex (pramipexole), developed in 1997 to treat Parkinson's disease, also works in treating patients with Restless Leg Syndrome (RLS), but it can cause amnesia. Amnesia is also a possible side effect of taking some cholesterol-lowering medications like Lipitor.

I get RLS at parent governor meetings when some parent launches into a rant. My leg starts twitching because it wants to get up and kick that person in the arse.

• Diane S. Aschenbrenner and Samantha J. Venable, Drug Therapy in Nursing, 3rd ed. (Lippincott Williams & Wilkins, 2008).

FACT: Some researchers believe that Mirapex leads to compulsive behaviours in some patients, turning occasional drinkers into alcoholics, casual card gamers or sports fans into compulsive gamblers, and otherwise normal people into hypersexuals, shopaholics, and binge eaters.

I don't know, that sounds kind of fun. I should ask my doctor if Mirapex is right for me.

• Allyson T. Collins, "Strange Side Effects Surprise Patients," ABC News, July 15, 2008, www.abcnews.com.

FACT: Patients who use Lipitor (atorvastatin) can be plagued by pain and weakness in their muscles, even to the point of loss of muscle control and coordination. Some patients have filed lawsuits against Lipitor's maker, Pfizer, stating that the drug causes permanent muscle damage, nerve damage, and memory loss.

The suit was dropped when the patients forgot that they were suing Pfizer and failed to show up for court.

• The PDR Pocket Guide to Prescription Drugs, 6th ed. (Simon & Schuster, 2003).
• Aaron Smith, "Pfizer Sued Over Alleged Lipitor Side Effects," June 8, 2006, CNNmoney, www.cnnmoney.com.

FACT: The drug Vasotec (enalapril) was developed to lower high blood pressure and treat congestive heart failure, but it can also have a detrimental effect on almost all of your senses, including loss of smell and taste, ringing in the ears (tinnitus), blurred vision, and dry eyes.

Dying has a detrimental effect on the senses, too, so take your pick.

• "Vasotec: Drug Description," RxList, www.rxlist.com.

 F A C T: Viagra (sildenafil), a treatment for erectile dysfunction, can cause blurred vision and problems distinguishing between green and blue. Researchers suspect that Viagra users are at risk of permanent loss of vision because the drug cuts off the flow of blood from the optic nerve, a condition called nonarteritic ischemic optic neuropathy (NAION).

I wonder where all that blood goes instead?

• "About Viagra," Viagra.com, www.viagra.com.
• "Viagra Can Cause Permanent Vision Loss in Some Men, University of Minnesota Researchers Say," Medical News Today, March 31, 2005, www.medicalnewstoday.com.

 F A C T: Many patients have reported suicidal thoughts while taking the antidepressant Paxil (paroxetine). Lawsuits allege that Paxil has severe withdrawal symptoms that, in some, resulted in suicide and attempted suicide. Evidence in one lawsuit shows GlaxoSmithKline, the drug's manufacturer, might have concealed data linking the drug to these effects.

'Paxil. I'd rather die than switch.'

• "FDA Statement Regarding the Anti-Depressant Paxil for Pediatric Population," FDA Talk Paper, U.S. Food and Drug Administration, June 19, 2003, www.fda.gov.
• "Glaxo Sued for 'Drug Claim Fraud'," BBCNews.com, June 2, 2004, www.howstuffworks.com.

 F A C T: Over 40 suicides and 400 suicide attempts are linked to Chantix (varenicline), an anti-smoking drug. The U.S. Department of Veterans Affairs has come under attack for recruiting soldiers who served in Iraq and Afghanistan as subjects in tests on Chantix after the FDA issued warnings about the drug's possible violent side effects.

They never said how Chantix stopped people from smoking, just that it could.

• Maddy Sauer and Vic Walter,"Tough Questions for VA on Suicide-Linked Chantix," ABCNews, July 8, 2008, www.abcnews.com.

FACT: The drug thalidomide is infamous for its link to birth defects. Though never proven to be safe, the drug was a popular sleeping aid and anti-nausea pill in the 1950s, taken by thousands of pregnant women. From 1956 to 1962, almost 10,000 women who were administered thalidomide delivered babies with phocomelia, a congenital disorder that causes children to be born with extremely short or missing limbs.

I'm guessing that their nausea and insomnia returned after those births.

• Michael J. O'Dowd, The History of Medications for Women: Materia Medica Woman (Informa Health Care, 2001), 249.

FACT: Accutane (isotretinoin), a drug used to treat severe acne, has also been linked to phocomelia. Women taking the drug have to adhere to a strict regimen to prevent becoming pregnant, including two methods of contraception and a required monthly blood test for pregnancy before a prescription refill is approved.

It's actually three methods of contraception, including the acne.

• Michael J. O'Dowd, The History of Medications for Women: Materia MedicaWoman (Informa Health Care, 2001).
• Paula Begoun, The Complete Beauty Bible: The Ultimate Guide to Smart Beauty (Rodale, 2004).

FACT: Half of all psychotherapists are threatened, harassed, or physically attacked by a patient, and up to 15 per cent of them have been stalked by former clients.

If they were better therapists, they wouldn't have this problem.

• Bryce Nelson, "Acts of Violence Against Therapists Pose Lurking Threat, New York Times, June 14, 1983.
• John C. Norcross and James D. Guy, Jr., Leaving It at the Office: A Guide to Psychotherapist Self-Care (Guilford Press, 2007), 44.

FACT: For centuries processed cockroaches have been used to cure ailments and physical disorders: cockroach tea has been used to treat dropsy (edema), an accumulation of fluid beneath the skin; fried cockroaches were used in African American folk medicine as a cure for indigestion; and cockroach poultice has been used to cure wounds and stingray burns.

Urgh, I'll just stick with paracetamol, thanks.

• Darrell Addison Posey and Kristina Plenderleith, Indigenous Knowledge and Ethics: A Darrell Posey Reader (Routledge, 2004).
• Marion Copeland, Cockroach (Reaktion Books, 2003).

 FACT: Urine therapy is the application of urine to the body through the skin or oral ingestion. Advocates drink a cup of their own urine every morning, which is to be sipped, not guzzled, and taken from 'midstream urine' collected in the morning. The treatment has been prescribed to stop chronic itching, soothe throat aches, and prevent cancer.

I'll just stick with scratching and gargling salt water, thanks.

• Flora Peschek-Böhmer and Gisela Schreiber, Urine Therapy: Nature's Elixir for Good Health (Inner Traditions / Bear & Company,1999).

 FACT: One seventeenth-century treatment for acne: chop the heads off two puppies, hang them by their heels to bleed, mix the collected blood with white wine, and apply the concoction to the face. A similar serum of 'Dog's Blood' was also once considered an effective treatment for tuberculosis.

Who came up with that treatment, a cat?

• Herbert P. Goodheart, Acne For Dummies (For Dummies, 2005).
• Boston Medical and Surgical Journal (Massachusetts Medical Society, 1892).

 FACT: Another folk remedy recommends rubbing earwax on cold sores or severely cracked lips to heal them.

Your own earwax, not someone else's. That would be disgusting.

• Elisabeth Janos, Country Folk Medicine: Tales of Skunk Oil, Sassafras Tea and Other Old-Time Remedies (Globe Pequot, 2004).

 FACT: Spiders were once thought to be an effective cure for malaria and were eaten alive in butter or in a spoonful of syrup. In India, spiderwebs were considered more effective, and were rolled into pellets and ingested orally.

As opposed to being ingested in some other way, which I prefer not to think about.

• Charles M. Poser and G. W.Bruyn, An Illustrated History of Malaria (Informa Health Care, 1999).

F A C T: In 2002, orthopedist David Arndt left the operating room seven hours into surgery so that he could cash his pay cheque before the bank closed. Arndt was gone for thirty-five minutes while the hospital paged him repeatedly. His medical license was later suspended.

Two words for you, Arndt: 'direct' and 'debit.'

• Neil Swidey, "What Went Wrong?," Boston Globe, March 21, 2004, www.boston.com.

F A C T: Obstetrician Dr Allan Zarkin made headlines in 2000 by carving his initials with a scalpel into a patient's stomach after delivering her baby by Caesarean section. Said Zarkin at the time, 'I did such a beautiful job, I'll initial it.' Zarkin was charged with assault and sued for malpractise by the patient.

Wow, a doctor did something obscenely arrogant. I'll alert the press.

• Jennifer Steinhauer, "Patient Settles Case Of Initials Cut in Skin," New York Times, February 12, 2000.
• Barbara Ross and Dave Goldiner, "Doctor Carved His Initials on New Mom," New York Daily News, January 21, 2000.

F A C T: An episiotomy is a surgical incision made below the vagina to assist childbirth. This common procedure is believed to lessen trauma to vaginal tissue, but it also carries a risk of numerous complications, including tearing of the rectum, bleeding, infection, extreme pain, and more. Some studies show that episiotomies cause more postpartum pain than not performing the procedure.

Imagine that.

• Melissa Conrad Stöpplerand William C. Shiel, Jr.,"Episiotomy," Medicinenet.com, December 9, 2008, www.medicinenet.com.

FACT: Though relatively common, Caesarean sections (C-sections) are major surgeries that deliver a baby through a mother's abdomen. A horizontal incision is made through the skin to the uterus. It poses risk to the health of the mother, including infection, injury to other organs, haemorrhage, complications from anesthesia, and a mortality rate for the mother that is twice to four times that of vaginal birth.

Other than that, it's a relatively simple and safe procedure.

• "Delivery Settings and Caesarean Section Rates in China," World Health Organization Bulletin, www.who.int.
• Rita Rubin, "Answers Prove Elusive as C-Section Rate Rises," USA Today, January 8, 2008, www.usatoday.com.
• "Cesarean Fact Sheet," Childbirth.org, www.childbirth.org.
• Robin Elise Weiss, "Cesarean Section Photos: Step-by-Step," About.com, www.pregnancy.about.com.
• Gerard M. DiLeo, "Your C-Section: A Step-by-Step Guide," Babyzone.com, www.babyzone.com.

FACT: In 1990, a sixty-three-year old woman went in for exploratory surgery on what doctors thought was a tumor on her buttock. They were wrong: the 'tumor' was a four-inch pork chop bone, which doctors estimated had been in place for five to ten years, but had not caused the woman any pain due to her obesity.

I like pork chops, too, but not enough to eat the bone.

• Worlds Most Incredible Stories (Barnes & Noble Publishing).

FACT: American women undergo twice as many hysterectomies as British women, and four times as many as Swedish women. By some estimates, 76–85 per cent of these procedures are unnecessary, studies saying that removing the ovaries will raise, not lower, her health risks unless a woman is highly at risk for ovarian cancer.

In most cases a woman is willing to take that chance if it means not having any more goddamn kids.

• Curt Pesmen, "Five Surgeriesto Avoid," Health, July 2007, updated September 18, 2008, www.living.health.com.

F A C T: Decompressive cranioplasty is an emergency surgery in which part of the cranium or skull is removed to reduce swelling of the brain. In some cases the removed bone fragment is stored in tissue of the abdominal wall and then reinserted into the skull several months later.

That bone fragment must be hell to swallow.

• T. Flannery and R. S. McConnell, "Cranioplasty: Why Throw the Bone Flap Out?" British Journal of Neurosurgery, December 2001, 518–520, www.informaworld.com.

F A C T: Blepharoplasty, or eye lift, is a surgical procedure that removes excess tissue to reshape the upper or lower eyelid. Risks of the surgery include asymmetry, cyst formation, and an inability to close the eye(s) due to excess skin removal.

Um, yeah, not being able to close your eyes? That's a problem.

• Neil Sadick and others, Concise Manual of Cosmetic Dermatologic Surgery (McGraw Hill Professional, 2007.
• John L. Wobig and Roger A. Dailey, Oculofacial Plastic Surgery: Face, Lacrimal System, and Orbit (Thieme, 2004).

F A C T: Surgical tools found in most operating rooms are similar to items you might find in a workshop, including saws, drills, chisels, and clamps. Other tools are the rongeur – French for 'gnawer' – a type of bone chisel, and retractors like the rib spreader, which uses a rack-and-pinion system to force apart ribs and tissue for surgical access to the internal cavity.

I apologise for this chapter. It wasn't my idea, I promise.

• Cynthia Spry, Essentials of Perioperative Nursing, 3rd ed. (Jones & Bartlett Publishers, 2005).
• "The Rib Spreader: A Chapter in the History of Thoracic Surgery," Chest, May 1972, 469–474.

F A C T: Queen Victoria eased the discomfort of her menstrual cramps with marijuana supplied by her doctor.

Even after menopause. Oops – she forgot to tell him.

• "Medical Marijuana," Canadian Foundation For Drug Policy, www.cfdp.ca.

F A C T: In the early 1900s, aspirin maker Bayer also commercially developed and sold heroin for several medicinal uses, including cough suppression.

I'm sure heroin suppresses many things.

• "Before Prohibition: Images from the Preprohibition Era when Many Psychotropic Substances Were Legally Available in America and Europe," University at Buffalo Department of Psychology, Addiction Research Unit, September 2001, www.wings.buffalo.edu.

F A C T: Office desks have 400 times more bacteria than toilet seats.

So, be safe and eat your lunch on a toilet instead of at your desk.

• "Average Desk Harbors 400 Times More Bacteria Than Average Toilet Seat," Medical-NewsService.com, March 31, 2002, www.medicalnewsservice.com.

F A C T: Telephones carry the most germs in an office, followed by desks, microwave doors, water fountain handles and computer keyboards.

You know what, just move your entire office into the toilets.

• "Average Desk Harbors 400 Times More Bacteria Than Average Toilet Seat," Medical-NewsService.com, March 31, 2002, www.medicalnewsservice.com.

F A C T: The place where you rest your hands on your desk is home to 10 million bacteria at any given time.

Well, not anymore. Seven million of them just moved to your hand.

• "Average Desk Harbors 400 Times More Bacteria Than Average Toilet Seat," Medical-NewsService.com, March 31, 2002, www.medicalnewsservice.com.

F A C T: An estimated 50,000 to 60,000 workers die every year from occupation related diseases.

Is not giving a shit considered an occupation-related disease? Because that affects a lot more than 60,000, I bet.

• "'Death on the Job' Report, 2008: The Toll of Neglect," American Federation of Labor – Congress of Industrial Organizations, www.aflcio.org.

FACT: Work-related stress can be as damaging to health as smoking cigarettes.

But if you handle that stress with a cigarette break, they cancel each other out.

• Natalie J. Jordet and Erica Lumiere, "Is Job Stress Making You Sick?," Marie Claire, www.marieclaire.com.

 FACT: The chronic stress of a high-pressure job has been shown to double the risk of a heart attack. Chronic stress may also result in alcoholism, hypertension, and severe depression, and can make your joints ache, your hair fall out, and even stop your period.

So that bald drunk lady at work who's always crying and giving away her tampons? Give her a break; she's under a lot of stress.

• Natalie J. Jordet and EricaLumiere, "Is Job Stress Making You Sick?," Marie Claire, www.marieclaire.com.

ALL CREATURES GREAT AND SMALL

Beastly tales in all shapes and sizes

F A C T: If you urinate when swimming in a South American river, you might encounter the candiru, a tiny fish that will follow a stream of urine to its source, enter the body, and flare its barbed fins, keeping it firmly embedded in the flesh until it can be surgically removed.

I need some of those in my pool.

• Ross Piper, Extraordinary Animals: An Encyclopedia of Curious and Unusual Animals (Greenwood Publishing Group, 2007).

F A C T: Electric eel cells can generate and release pulses of more than 500 volts.

Scientists are hoping to use these cells to power medical equipment, which sounds like something out of The Flintstones: your sleep apnoea machine stops, you open a compartment on the side, and there's an eel with his feet up, smoking. 'What? I'm on a break!' he says.

• Eric Bland, "Electric Eel Cells Inspire Energy Source," Discovery Channel, www.dsc.discovery.com.

F A C T: The sea lizard is a type of sea slug that will eat venomous cnidarians like the Portuguese Man of War, swallowing its stinging cells whole, and collecting them in its outer extremities to act as a defense against predators.

Sea lizards are such users.

• Edmund D. Brodie and John D. Dawson, Poisonous Animals (Macmillan, 2001).

 F A C T: One of the most venomous marine creatures in the world is the box jellyfish. It can kill a human within minutes by uncoiling and firing its stinging tentacles into the victim, then pumping venom through the tentacles to paralyze him and cause cardiac arrest.

If I were a box jellyfish, I'd work on getting a more hardcore name. 'Box jellyfish' sounds like something you'd get for lunch on a school trip.

• "The 10 Most Dangerous Animals in the World," AOL Travel, www.travel.aol.co.uk.

 F A C T: The Australian blue-ringed octopus has potent venomous saliva that can cause numbness, paralysis, and death in humans.

I once saw a nature program on TV that described the octopus as 'affectionate.' I don't think they were talking about this one.

• Edmund D. Brodie and John D. Dawson, Poisonous Animals (Macmillan, 2001).

 F A C T: The stingray uses a serrated spine on the upper surface of its tail to lash and cut into victims, injecting them with venom. Stings are intensely painful, and cause decreased blood pressure and erratic heart rate.

At least they don't bury themselves in the sand and wait for you to step on them so they can sting you. Oh, wait, yes they do.

• Edmund D. Brodie and John D. Dawson, Poisonous Animals (Macmillan, 2001).

 F A C T: When threatened, the sea cucumber ejects sticky, long threads from its body to ensnare predators. Some species will contract their bodies, violently expelling internal organs that contain a deadly toxin.

The sea onion, on the other hand, just falls apart and cries.

- "The Sea Cucumber," How Stuff Works, www.animals.howstuffworks.com.
- "Sea Cucumber," National Geographic, Animals, http://animals.nationalgeographic.com.

 FACT: Up to 30 per cent of Britain's rats carry Weil's disease, which can be fatal to humans.

They're the ones toting little boxes and acting suspiciously.

- "The UK's Deadliest Creatures," AOL Travel, www.travel.aol.co.uk

 FACT: A rat can compress its body to fit through an opening as small as half an inch in diameter, making it almost impossible to rat-proof a building or home.

I once compressed a rat even smaller than that – with a spade.

- "The UK's Deadliest Creatures," AOL Travel, www.travel.aol.co.uk.
- "Norway Rats," Illinois Department of Public Health: Prevention & Control, www.idph.state.il.us.

 FACT: Male desert rats can copulate up to 150 times in an afternoon.

God, I miss uni.

- Edward G. Long, Chimpanzees Don't Wear Pants: A Retired Psychiatrist Takes a Second Look at Human Nature (Buy Books On The Web, 2001).

 FACT: Ursodiol, a compound made from bear bile, is used in Western medicine to dissolve gallstones and treat cirrhosis of the liver.

Getting the bile – that's the tricky part.

- Constanza Villalba, "Ten Lessons Medicine Can Learn from Bears," Scientific American, January 6, 2009, www.sciam.com.

 FACT: Of the world's numerous species of bears, the most deadly are polar, black, and grizzly bears. These species will attack, trample, and maul their prey until it is frightened off or dead, and will attack for a variety of reasons, including hunger.

Or simply to impress their bear friends. 'Hey, guys – watch me scare the shit

out of this tourist.'

• "The 10 Most Dangerous Animals in the World," AOL Travel, www.travel.aol.co.uk.

 F A C T: The small but venomous saw-scaled viper causes more deaths in North Africa and the Middle East than any other snake. When attacked, it can hurl its body at an aggressor and bite quickly.

That's exactly how I fight. They never expect the biting.

• Ted Mertens and Helen Lucas, Deadly & Dangerous Snakes (Magic Bean, 1995).

 F A C T: If cornered, some horned lizard species can shoot blood from their eye sockets up to distances of six feet. Though not toxic, the blood has a foul taste, particularly to canine predators like coyotes and foxes.

You know, if I corner something that wants to live so badly that it's willing to shoot blood from its eyes, I'd spare it just on principle.

• Wade C. Sherbrooke, Introduction to Horned Lizards of North America (University of California Press, 2003).

 F A C T: Cone shells are a dangerous type of snail with hollow, venom-filled teeth that it can shoot like darts at its victims. Their deadly venom causes paralysis and can sometimes kill humans within minutes.

Killed by a snail – that would be rubbish. I need to ask my wife to lie for me if that ever happens, tell people I ate it hang-gliding or climbing Mt. Everest or something cool. Not by a snail.

• Edmund D. Brodie and John D. Dawson, Poisonous Animals (Macmillan, 2001).

 F A C T: When threatened, the hairy frog, or 'horror frog,' intentionally breaks its own bones to produce claws that puncture through the frog's toe pads to become defensive weapons.

I liked frogs better when they just peed in your hand and gave you warts.

• "Top 10 Deadliest Animals," LIVEScience, www.livescience.com.
• "Ten of the Most Bizarre Animal Defense Mechanisms," WebEcoist, November 4, 2008, www.webecoist.com.

F A C T: A tiger shark's bite is powerful enough to slice through a hard turtle shell.

That doesn't mean that they will. That's a lot of work for a little bit of meat – a bit like crab legs.

• Mark Carwardine, Shark (Firefly Books, 2004).

F A C T: In some species of sharks, embryos are cannibalistic, feeding on each other in the womb until only the strongest shark remains.

Sibling rivalry starts early. 'Where's your brother? And what's in your mouth?'

•Walter Sullivan, "In Shark Womb, Fetus 'Cannibalizes' Rivals," New York Times, December 7, 1982, www.nytimes.com.

F A C T: A zorilla, or striped polecat, is a type of weasel that resembles a skunk, and is arguably the world's smelliest animal. If threatened, the zorilla ejects a powerful, foul-smelling fluid from its anus into the face of its assailant with impressive accuracy.

Babies can do that, too.

• Robert Burton, International Wildlife Encyclopedia, 3rd ed. (Marshall Cavendish, 2002).
• "Ictonyx Striatus," University Of Michigan Museum Of Zoology, www.animaldiversity.ummz.umich.edu.

F A C T: An adult tiger can kill its prey with a single bite, and can eat a large amounts of food – up to 180 lbs – in just a few days.

Whew. I'm safe.

• Valmik Thapar, Land of the Tiger: A Natural History of the Indian Subcontinent (University of California Press, 1997).

F A C T: A giraffe has twelve-inch hooves and legs that can kick in all four directions with incredible power. Giraffe kicks have been known to decapitate lions.

I bet lions hate that.

• Lynn Sherr, Tall Blondes: A Book about Giraffes (Andrews McMeel, 1997).

F A C T: Female marsupials have three vaginal openings, and males have a bifurcated, or forked, penis.

There's a limerick in there somewhere.

• Luis P. Villarreal, Viruses and the Evolution of Life (ASM Press, 2005).

F A C T: In 2009, a 200-pound chimpanzee attacked an elderly Connecticut woman, crushing her hands and ripping large chunks from her scalp, face, jaw, and eyes. Medics at first had trouble determining if the victim was a man or a woman.

Did it really matter at that point?

• "Some Injuries Too Much Even for Doctors to Handle Alone," ABCNews.com, February 24, 2009, www.abcnews.go.com.

F A C T: Elephants may appear friendly and approachable, but don't be fooled: these unpredictable giants cause an estimated 300–500 fatalities a year. Even tame, trained elephants have been known to attack without provocation and kill zookeepers who have been with them for as long as fifteen years.

Elephant to her psychiatrist: 'I tried to forget all the hurtful things he said to me over the years, but I couldn't.'

• "The 10 Most Dangerous Animals in the World," AOL Travel, www.travel.aol.co.uk.

F A C T: In 1972, the Chandka Forest area in India was hit by a heat wave so brutal, it caused herds of elephants to stampede through five villages, leaving a trail of devastation and twenty-four fatalities.

And nobody heard them coming?

• David Wallechinsky, The New Book of Lists: The Original Compendium of Curious Information (Canon gate U.S., 2005), 307.

F A C T: The hippopotamus is a highly aggressive animal, and one of Africa's most deadly. Hippos will charge, trample, and gore victims with alarming ferocity, and have upended boats and canoes to feast on victims inside, despite being herbivores.

They're sensitive about their weight, and the whole 'hungry, hungry hippo' thing makes them furious.

• "The 10 Most Dangerous Animals in the World," AOL Travel, www.travel.aol.co.uk.

 F A C T: Crocodiles are ferocious killers that cause 600–800 deaths every year. Crocs attack with terrifying speed, launching themselves out of the water to snare prey, which they drag underwater and spin repeatedly in a death roll until the victim is drowned or too disoriented to fight back.

Deathroll – sounds like something a crocodile would order at a sushi bar.

• "The 10 Most Dangerous Animals in the World," AOL Travel, www.travel.aol.co.uk.

 F A C T: If a swan hisses at you, take heed. Swans have been known to capsize boats, attack humans on jet skis, and strangle dogs to death. They kill by holding their victim's head under the water until it drowns.

I think I just found a new prey species for crocodiles.

• "The 10 Most Dangerous Animals in the World," AOL Travel, www.travel.aol.co.uk.
• "The UK's Deadliest Creatures," AOL Travel, www.travel.aol.co.uk.

 F A C T: A polar bear can rip the head off a human with one swipe of its paw.

My mum could do that with just a look.

• "Top 10 Deadliest Animals," LIVEScience, www.livescience.com.

 F A C T: The skunk's anal musk is so powerful that it can cause temporary blindness if sprayed directly into the eyes.

Sounds a lot like my Uncle Phil. His anal musk could make your hair bleed.

• "Ten of the Most Bizarre Animal Defense Mechanisms," WebEcoist, November 4, 2008, www.webecoist.com.

 F A C T: If cornered, an opossum can foam at the mouth to convince a predator that it is toxic or sick, or discharge an anal fluid that smells almost as bad as a skunk's spray.

Unfortunately, neither of these works on a speeding car.

• "Ten of the Most Bizarre Animal Defense Mechanisms," WebEcoist, November 4, 2008, www.webecoist.com.

 FACT: A dead whale spontaneously exploded while in transit on a truck in 2004. Internal pressure caused by methane gas build up within the body was identified as the cause.

I'm sure that smelled wonderful.

• "A Brief History of Actual Exploding Animals," WebEcoist, September 5th, 2008, www.webecoist.com.

 FACT: A resurgent wild turkey population caused problems in Boston in 2008, chasing joggers and schoolchildren, often in large mobs of birds.

Note to Boston: wild turkey is edible.

• Tim Dowling, "A Beginner's Guide to Beating off these Vicious Predators," The Guardian, May 13, 2008, www.guardian.co.uk.

 FACT: The largest predatory fish in the world is the great white shark. They average fifteen feet in length, though great whites as long as twenty feet have been documented. Over 100 shark attacks occur worldwide each year and 30–50 per cent of them are caused by great whites. The great white can also swim up to 15 mph.

Know what can't? You.

• "Great White Shark Profile," National Geographic, www.animals.nationalgeographic.com.

 FACT: The black mamba is considered the world's deadliest snake. Territorial and aggressive, the black mamba strikes repeatedly to kill its prey with powerful venom. One of Africa's longest venomous snakes, the mamba can grow up to fourteen feet long, and is also among the fastest snakes in the world, moving at up to twelve and a half miles per hour.

What, no wings?

• "Snakes," National Geographic, www.animals.nationalgeographic.com.
• "Snakebit: Surviving The Black Mamba," ABC News, www.abcnews.go.com.

F A C T: Pigs can become alcoholics.

No. Too easy.

• FactLib.com, www.factlib.com.

 F A C T: Two snakes cause more human deaths than any others in the world: the Russell's viper and the spectacled cobra, named for the eyeglass design on its flared hood. Both are extremely venomous and found in highly populated areas in Southeast Asia.

Highly populated for now, that is.

• "Snakes," Photo Gallery, National Geographic, www.animals.nationalgeographic.com

 F A C T: The cassowary is the world's most dangerous bird: it weighs over a 100 lbs, can run 30mph, and jump over three feet high. New Guinea tribesmen use the cassowary's sharp claws as spearheads. Attacks on humans have resulted in broken bones and even death.

Why aren't we eating these things?

• Brendan Borrell, "Invasion of the Cassowaries," Smithsonian Magazine, October 2008, www.smithsonianmag.com.

 F A C T: A cockroach carries more than forty different pathogens that can be transferred to humans, including pneumonia, hepatitis, and typhoid.

I have a pathogen that can be transferred to cockroaches. It's called the bottom of my shoe, and it is fatal 100 per cent of the time.

• Greta Garbage, That's Disgusting!: An Adult Guide to What's Gross, Tasteless, Rude, Crude, and Lewd (Ten Speed Press,1999).

 F A C T: Because of its high food intake, a housefly deposits faeces constantly – about every five minutes – which makes it a carrier of more than 100 disease-causing agents.

And you thought that babies shat a lot.

• Yiu H. Hui, Handbook of Food Science, Technology, and Engineering (CRC Press, 2006).

F A C T: The colour of a head louse tends to mimic the colour of the person's hair in which it lives, making it more difficult to detect.

After years of poor service, Bob was named Head Louse of his department.

• May R. Berenbaum, Bugs in the System: Insects and Their Impact on Human Affairs (Basic Books, 1996).

 F A C T: Aphids are born impregnated, do not require sex to procreate, and can give birth within a week of being born themselves, making them prolific. In large numbers, aphids can cause serious damage to crops.

Probably because they aren't getting any sex.

• Jerry Baker, Jerry Baker's Bug Off!: 2,193 Super Secrets for Battling Bad Bugs, Outfoxing Crafty Critters, Evicting Voracious Varmints and Much More! (American Master Products, 2005).
• Denny Schrock, Home Gardener's Problem Solver: Symptoms and Solutions for More Than 1,500 Garden Pests and Plant Ailments, 3rd ed. (Ortho Books, 2004).

 F A C T: There are about 10 quintillion insects on Earth at any given moment; that's 1.5 billion insects for every human on the planet.

One and a half billion bugs? Sounds like Windows 7.

• Jerry Baker, Jerry Baker's Bug Off!: 2,193 Super Secrets for Battling Bad Bugs, Outfoxing Crafty Critters, Evicting Voracious Varmints and Much More! (American Master Products, 2005).

 F A C T: The Vespa mandarinia japonica, or Japanese giant hornet, is the size of your thumb, has a painful sting, and can spray flesh-melting poison into your eyes. Its poison also contains a pheromone that can summon every hornet in the hive to attack.

At least they don't overdo it.

• Ross Piper, Extraordinary Animals: An Encyclopedia of Curious and Unusual Animals (Greenwood Publishing Group, 2007).

 F A C T: As the world's most venomous insect per sting, the Japanese giant hornet kills forty people every year, all of them excruciatingly painful.

What, all that stinging and flesh-melting and hive-summoning, and they only manage forty kills a year?

• Ross Piper, Extraordinary Animals: An Encyclopedia of Curious and Unusual Animals (Greenwood Publishing Group, 2007).

 F A C T: Africanized honey bees, better known as 'killer bees,' hail from South and Central America, and as of 2006, were established in the American South and Southwest. Killer bees are extremely aggressive and prone to potentially deadly attacks when disturbed.

I'm the same way when I'm on the toilet and my kids try to come in.

• John L. Capinera, Encyclopedia of Entomology, 2nd ed. (Springer, 2008).

 F A C T: Killer bees are extremely territorial and have a propensity for mass stinging attacks on both humans and animals. Swarms can kill any number of humans from a few dozen people in Mexico to several hundred in Venezuela.

I'd like to see killer bees and Japanese hornets fight it out.

• John L. Capinera, Encyclopedia of Entomology, 2nd ed. (Springer, 2008).

 F A C T: There is no physical way to determine the difference between an Africanized honey bee and the less harmful European bee – even a specialist must examine several bees together to differentiate them.

Can't you just ask them?

• John L. Capinera, Encyclopedia of Entomology, 2nd ed. (Springer, 2008).

 F A C T: Army ants are half an inch in length and notorious for dismantling any living thing in their path, regardless of its size, thanks to massive, machete-like jaws that are half the size of their own bodies.

Army ants are also known as Hilary Swank ants.

• Ken Preston-Mafham, The Encyclopedia of Land Invertebrate Behaviour (MIT Press, 1993).

 F A C T: Army ants attack cows and horses by swarming up their legs and attacking the soft tissue of the eyes and nose. If assaulted while penned in, these animals can become so hysterical that they will beat themselves to death trying to escape.

I feel the same way at my in-laws'.

• Alzada Carlisle Kistner, An Affair with Africa: Expeditions and Adventures Across a Continent (Island Press, 1998).
• Ken Preston-Mafham, The Encyclopedia of Land Invertebrate Behaviour (MIT Press, 1993).

 F A C T: Human botfly larva can grow anywhere in the body, and have been removed from the head, arms, back, abdomen, buttocks, thighs, and armpits of humans. They can even penetrate the incompletely ossified skull of a young child and burrow into the brain.

There had better not be a human scrotum botfly.

• Jerome Goddard, Physician's Guide to Arthropods of Medical Importance, 5th ed. (CRC Press, 2007).

 F A C T: Kissing bugs usually prey on bed bugs but will suck blood from humans, too. They earn their sweet name in a not-so-sweet way: by biting the lips, eyelids, and ears of sleeping human victims, causing intense pain that can last weeks or even months.

Kissing bugs are not the same as Arse-Kissing bugs, which do not bite but will continuously lick and nibble the hindquarters of anyone in authority.

• Howard Garrett and C. Malcolm Beck, Texas Bug Book: The Good, the Bad, and the Ugly, 2nd ed. (University of Texas Press, 2005).

 F A C T: Bee assassin insects have hairs on their legs that allow them to catch and hold onto their prey. Though named for their penchant for killing bees, assassins are opportunistic and attack many other insects, immobilizing prey with a powerful, fast-acting toxin. Their bite is more painful to humans than bee and wasp stings.

You've probably heard of would-be assassins, but not bee assassins. Don't confuse would-be assassins with insects aspiring to become bee assassins; those are called would-be bee assassins.

• Maurice Burton and Robert Burton, International Wildlife Encyclopedia, 3rd ed. (Marshall Cavendish, 2002).

F A C T: The most dangerous insect in the world is the mosquito, responsible for the spread of malaria, which infects 350–500 million people each year, killing as many as a million.

I thought that most of them lived in my back garden.

• Eric R. Eaton and Kenn Kaufman, Kaufman Field Guide to Insects of North America (Houghton Mifflin Harcourt, 2007).
• "Malaria," Centres for Disease Control and Prevention, www.cdc.gov.
• American Mosquito Control Association, www.mosquito.org.

F A C T: When biting prey, Brazilian wandering spiders inject up to .003 ounces of powerful venom, an amount strong enough to kill 300 mice.

What do you call 300 dead mice on the jungle floor? A good start.

• Robert S. Anderson, Richard Beatty, and Stuart Church, Insects and Spiders of the World (Marshall Cavendish, 2003).

F A C T: Jumping spiders hunt by stalking and leaping on victims while trailing a safety line of silk behind them. Their eight eyes give them almost 180-degree vision, and they can jump up to twenty times their own length.

Because regular old walking spiders weren't creepy enough.

• Paul Hillyard, The Private Life of Spiders (New Holland Publishers, 2007).

F A C T: The Sydney funnel-web spider is Australia's most dangerous arachnid, with a bite capable of causing death in fifteen minutes.

Just try not to get bitten until the end of your trip, because Sydney is a great city and I recommend seeing as much of it as you can before you die. Especially since you probably won't be returning.

• Jerome Goddard, Physician's Guide to Arthropods of Medical Importance, 5th ed. (CRC Press, 2007).

F A C T: It has no bite, but the common housefly is one of the world's most deadly insects, thanks to the long list of diseases that it carries and spreads: typhoid, cholera, gangrene, tuberculosis, smallpox, bubonic plague, diphtheria, dysentery, and more.

Bubonic plague? That shit's still around?!

• Leland Ossian Howard, The House Fly, Disease Carrier: An Account of Its Dangerous Activities and of the Means of Destroying It, 3rd ed. (Frederick A. Stokes, 1911).

 F A C T: An individual housefly can carry up to 33 million bacteria on the outer surface of its body, 6 million on its feet alone.

For this reason, you should always insist that a housefly wipes its feet before entering your home.

• Leland Ossian Howard, The House Fly, Disease Carrier: An Account of Its Dangerous Activities and of the Means of Destroying It, 3rd ed. (Frederick A. Stokes, 1911).
• Julie J. Shaffner, Kasey Jo Warner, and W. Wyatt Hoback, Filth Flies: Experiments to Test Flies as Vectors of Bacterial Disease (The American Biology Teacher Online, Feb 2007).

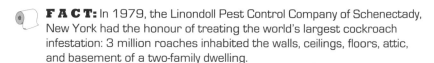 **F A C T:** In 1979, the Linondoll Pest Control Company of Schenectady, New York had the honour of treating the world's largest cockroach infestation: 3 million roaches inhabited the walls, ceilings, floors, attic, and basement of a two-family dwelling.

Sounds more like two families inhabited a 3-million roach dwelling.

• Mark L. Winston, Nature Wars: People Vs. Pests (Harvard University Press, 1999).

 F A C T: There are 4,000 species of cockroach in the world, 95 per cent of them able to survive completely independent of humans.

We'd get along just fine without them, too.

• Jerome Goddard, Physician's Guide to Arthropods of Medical Importance, 5th ed. (CRC Press, 2007).

 F A C T: A cockroach can survive for several weeks without a head.

Yes, but it spends those weeks bumping into walls and screaming, 'Where the FUCK is my head?!'

• Jerome Goddard, Physician's Guide to Arthropods of Medical Importance, 5th ed. (CRC Press, 2007).

 F A C T: In Africa, cattle bitten by the O. savignyi breed of tick may die of toxicosis in just one day.

Just before the animal dies, it makes a horrible grimace that researchers

call the 'O. savignyi Face,' or 'O Face' for short.

• Jerome Goddard, Physician's Guide to Arthropods of Medical Importance, 5th ed. (CRC Press, 2007).

F A C T: Hundreds of pets and livestock are injured or killed by tick paralysis, a result of bites from certain breeds of ticks. The severity of the paralysis depends on the number of female tick bites received by the host.

Of course it does. Weaker sex, my arse.

• Jerome Goddard, Physician's Guide to Arthropods of Medical Importance, 5th ed. (CRC Press, 2007).

F A C T: There are 1,250 species of scorpions in the world, on every continent but Antarctica. Their toxic stings can result in abdominal cramps, blurred vision, partial paralysis, abnormal eye movements, priapism (persistent erection), hypertension, tachycardia, convulsions, and death from respiratory paralysis.

Aside from the priapism, scorpion bites sound like a drag.

• Jerome Goddard, Physician's Guide to Arthropods of Medical Importance, 5th ed. (CRC Press, 2007).
• "Priapism," Merriam-Webster Online Dictionary, www.merriam-webster.com.

F A C T: The seemingly harmless ladybird has been known to inflict unprovoked bites and release a defensive secretion that causes a stinging sensation on human skin.

Not very ladylike, if you ask me.

• Jerome Goddard, Physician's Guide to Arthropods of Medical Importance, 5th ed. (CRC Press, 2007).

F A C T: Many parasitic worms use beetles as intermediate hosts to get to humans. One case reported an 8cm worm found in a baby's nappy; the infant had presumably ingested an infected beetle via contaminated flour or bread products.

If you've ever changed a shitty nappy, there's really nothing you could find in there that would surprise you – a worm, a frog, Lord Lucan, whatever.

• Jerome Goddard, Physician's Guide to Arthropods of Medical Importance, 5th ed. (CRC Press, 2007).

F A C T: When threatened, blister beetles secrete a chemical that will produce a sore within a few hours of penetrating the skin. This chemical agent is poisonous to some animal species, and, when ingested, can lead to abdominal pain, kidney damage, and even death.

The blister beetle will also secrete some chemicals when stamped into smithereens by my foot, which is what will happen to any beetle that gives me a blister.

• Jerome Goddard, Physician's Guide to Arthropods of Medical Importance, 5th ed. (CRC Press, 2007).

F A C T: It would take 500–800 honey bee stings to kill a human based on the toxic effects of the venom alone, but to someone with a bee allergy, one sting can cause a deadly anaphylactic reaction.

If you get stung 500–800 times by bees, you need better trainers.

• Jerome Goddard, Physician's Guide to Arthropods of Medical Importance, 5th ed. (CRC Press, 2007).

F A C T: Long-term lice infection of humans can result in what's known as secondary sensitisation, or a feeling of apathy, pessimism, or irritability, hence the expression, 'feeling lousy.'

Long-term lice infection of a human can also result in what's known as never having a relationship, ever. This also creates a feeling of apathy, irritability, pessimism, and chronic virginity.

• Jerome Goddard, Physician's Guide to Arthropods of Medical Importance, 5th ed. (CRC Press, 2007).

F A C T: The praying mantis will eat its own kind. The most famous example of this is the female's notorious mating behaviour where she sometimes eats the male just after – or even during – mating.

Whether it's after or during depends largely on how good he is in the sack.

• "Praying Mantis," Animals, National Geographic, http://animals.nationalgeographic.com.

ARE YOU GONNA EAT THAT?

The ugly truth about food and drink

 FACT: Bottled drinking water has been marketed as being cleaner and more pure than tap water, but, in a recent study, a third of bottled water showed significant chemical or bacterial contamination, including arsenic, nitrates, carcinogenic compounds, and coliform bacteria.

Probably the bottom third; that kind of stuff tends to sink.

• "Bottled Water: Pure Drink or Pure Hype?" National Resources Defense Council, www.nrdc.org.

 FACT: Bottled water is rarely tested for purity. An Environmental Working Group study found that ten popular brands were riddled with chemical pollutants and bacteria, some as high as tap water.

Hey, you wanted low prices.

• "FDA Should Adopt EPA Tap Water Health Goals for Bottled Water," news release, Environmental Working Group, November 19, 2008, www.ewg.org.
• "Bottled Water: Pure Drink or Pure Hype?" National Resources Defense Council, www.nrdc.org.

FACT: While the results of tap water contamination tests are made public, manufacturers of bottled water do not divulge their test results.

Chalk it up to the protection of trade secrets. Every brand of bottled water has its own proprietary blend of pathogens, contaminants, and waste that give the product its uniquely refreshing taste.

• "FDA Should Adopt EPA Tap Water Health Goals for Bottled Water," news release, Environmental Working Group, November 19, 2008, www.ewg.org.

F A C T: According to government and industry estimates, almost 40 per cent of bottled water is ordinary tap water, often with no additional treatment.

'Additional treatment' = changing the lawn hose before filling a new batch.

• "FDA Should Adopt EPA Tap Water Health Goals for Bottled Water," news release, Environmental Working Group, November 19, 2008, www .ewg.org.
• "Bottled Water: Pure Drink or Pure Hype?" National Resources Defense Council, www.nrdc.org.

F A C T: One pound of peanut butter can contain up to 150 insect fragments and 5 rodent hairs.

Up to 150? That means there could only be 120–130. Whew! I was almost disgusted there for a second.

• Stephanie Bailey, "Bug Food:Edible Insects," University of Kentucky College of Agriculture, Entomology Department, www.ca.uky.edu.
• "Food Defect Action Levels," U.S. Food and Drug Administration Centre for Food Safety and Applied Nutrition, last updated November 2005, www.cfsan.fda.gov.

F A C T: One in five office coffee mugs contains faecal bacteria and E. coli, which can cause diarrhoea, food poisoning, and infections.

Not surprising, since most office coffee tastes like shit. Related fact: Three of five office coffee mugs feature sayings that are meant to be funny but aren't, like 'Bean me up, Scotty' and 'No coffee, no workee.'

• Stephanie Muller, "Stay Healthy with Tips from a Germ Freak," Health Communications Quarterly, October 19, 2005, www.usjt.com.
• "Dr. Germ," Information for News Media, University of Arizona College of Agricultural and Life Sciences, February 17, 2005, www.cals.arizona.edu.

F A C T: Vegetarians beware: many low-fat and non-fat yogurts and sweets contain gelatin, which is made from animal tendons, ligaments, and bones.

You'd think the crunching would give it away. It must be drowned out by the sound of all those vegetarians patting themselves on the back for being vegetarians.

• Ayami Chin, "Gross Facts You May Have Never Wanted to Know," Associated Content, May 24, 2007, www.associatedcontent.com.
• Ernest R. Vieira and Louis J. Ronsivalli, Elementary Food Science, 4thed. (Springer, 1999), 237.
• Audrey Ensminger, Foods and Nutrition Encyclopedia, 2nd ed. (CRC Press, 1994), 1057.

 F A C T: Fining is a process used by most wineries to remove particles and impurities from wine. Typical fining agents include isinglass (a collagen from sturgeon bladders), gelatin, and ox blood.

Whatever impurities are removed by fining, are they worse than fish urine, animal bones and ox blood?

• Thor Iverson, "Ladybug Marmalade," Stuff Boston, January 12, 2009, www.stuffboston.com.
• Emile Peynaud, Knowing and Making Wine, trans. Alan Spencer, 2nd ed. (Wiley-IEEE, 1984), 291–294.

 F A C T: Even when grapes are harvested by hand, some insects wind up in the pickers' baskets. Workers simply don't have time to inspect every grape individually as they work.

Consider it fibre. We all need fibre.

• Thor Iverson, "Ladybug Marmalade," Stuff Boston, January 12, 2009, www.stuffboston.com.
• G. L. Creasy, G. I. Creasey, and Leroy L. Creasy, Grapes (CABI, 2009), 180.

 F A C T: Most wines are made from grapes harvested by machines that scythe through everything in their path, including sticks, insects, rodents, and even larger mammals, which can make their way into the end product. This is known to wine growers as MOG, or 'material other than grapes.'

MOG also stands for 'Mother of God, I think that was a hoof.'

• Thor Iverson, "Ladybug Marmalade," Stuff Boston, January 12, 2009, www.stuffboston.com.
• Ronald S. Jackson, Wine Science: Principles and Applications, 3rd ed. (Academic Press, 2008),
• John Smith, "Grapes: MOG," Oakstone Winery, www.oakstone-winery.com.

F A C T: In 2001, the Ontario, Canada wine region was hit by an infestation of ladybirds, which infiltrated many area wineries. When agitated, ladybirds secrete a strong, foul liquid containing pyrazine, a flavour similar to rancid peanuts – and one that was perceptible in numerous wines of that vintage.

Rancid Pinot Noir and Bugjolais, for example.

• Thor Iverson, "Ladybug Marmalade,"Stuff Boston, January 12, 2009, www.stuffboston.com.
• "Ladybug, Ladybug, Get Outta My Wine," Canadian Broadcasting Centre News, January 28, 2003, www.cbc.ca.

 F A C T: Moulds are tiny organisms with thread-like roots that burrow deep into the foods where they grow. While some moulds are safe, like those used to make certain kinds of cheese – Roquefort, Gorgonzola, Brie – most moulds are unsafe for consumption, as they can contain listeria, brucella, salmonella and E. coli.

Mould is also used to make Frumunda, a briny, piquant cheese from the Nether regions of Crackoslovokia.

• Katherine Zeratsky, "Mouldy Cheese: Is it unsafe to eat?" Nutrition and Healthy Eating, Expert Answers, Mayo Clinic, www.mayoclinic.com.

 F A C T: Parasitic round worms such as Anisakis simplex, frequently found in fish, can lead to anisakiasis in humans, a condition marked by severe abdominal and gastric pain, nausea, vomiting and abdominal distention, which can last for months.

I think my wife's been cooking with those.

• R. Wootten and D. C. Cann,"Round Worms in Fish," Food and Agriculture Association of the United Nations, Ministry of Agriculture Fisheries and Food, Torry Research Station, www.fao.org.
• Sari Edelstein and others, Food and Nutrition at Risk in America:Food Insecurity, Biotechnology, Food Safety, and Bioterrorism (Jones & Bartlett, 2008), 28.

 F A C T: Corn is in almost everything we consume. It is the primary food for the chicken, pigs, and cows that we eat; the source of corn oils found in many snack foods, margarines, and baked goods; used to make high-fructose corn syrup, the most prevalent, cheapest and, some believe, most hazardous of all sweeteners; and the source of food additives.

As a result, corn is found in things that come out of our bodies, too. Like the one you're working on right now.

• Melissa Diane Smith, "Corn Fed and Fat: The American Problem That is Spreading to Other Countries," News & Notes, Against the Grain Nutrition, July 31, 2008, www.againstthegrainnutrition.com
• Audrey Ensminger, Foods and Nutrition Encyclopedia, 2nd ed. (CRC Press, 1994).

FACT: Many environmentalists believe that salmon farms could have a catastrophic effect on the world's wild salmon populations. Concentrations of solid waste and nitrogens from farmed pens can poison marine life, and many researchers fear that salmon farm escapees could soon overrun and decimate wild stocks.

Although farmers use dogfish to track the escapees, most ultimately find their way to freedom. Fish that are caught are returned to the farms, where they face intense grilling over an open flame for 8–10 minutes.

• David F. Arnold and William (FRW) Cronan, The Fishermen's Frontier: People and Salmon in Southeast Alaska (University of Washington Press, 2008), 187.

FACT: Peaches, apples, nectarines, and strawberries are among the top six 'dirtiest' foods, according to investigations by the Environmental Working Group. More than 90 per cent of samples of these fruits tested positive for detectable pesticides, even after being rinsed or peeled.

What, that two-second splash of cold water didn't wash off the chemicals?

• "Shopper's Guide to Pesticides," The Environmental Working Group, www.foodnews.org.

FACT: Red-coloured food items like strawberry yogurt are often dyed with carmine, which is made from ground-up cochineal beetles. For some, carmine can cause severe allergic reactions and can even lead to anaphylactic shock.

That's a shame, because eating ground-up beetles sounds really good otherwise.

• Daniel M. Marmion, Handbook of U.S. Colourants: Foods, Drugs, Cosmetics, and Medical Devices, 3rd ed. (Wiley-Interscience, 1991), 128.

• J.B. Greig, "Cochineal Extract, Carmine, and Carminic Acid," WHO Food Additive Series 46, Food Standards Agency, London, www.inchem.org.

FACT: Mushrooms can kill. The two species most commonly to blame in mushroom poisonings are the Death Cap, which contains seven toxins and can be lethal with just one bite, and the Destroying Angel, often confused for an edible white cap mushroom.

Death Cap. Destroying Angel. Who names these things, Dr Evil?

• Dahlia Rideout, "Ten Dangerous & Deadly Foods," Divine Caroline, www.divinecaroline.com.
• Ian Robert Hall, Edible and Poisonous Mushrooms of the World (Timber Press, 2003).

FACT: Think that you're avoiding monosodium glutamate (MSG) by checking product labels? You could be wrong. Food makers now conceal MSG in packaged foods by listing it under other names, such as autolyzed or hydrolyzed vegetable protein, torula yeast, soy extracts, yeast extract, and protein isolate.

So the next time you're at a Chinese restaurant, instead of asking for 'No MSG, please,' say, 'No autolyzed or hydrolyzed vegetable protein, torula yeast, soy extracts, yeast extract, and protein isolate, please.' And the waiter will still nod and smile as if the MSG wasn't already in the food and he could remove it even if he had any intention of doing so, which he doesn't.

• Mike Adams, "Grocery Warning: The Seven Most Dangerous Ingredients in Conventional Foods,"(Truth Publishing LLC, 2006), Organic Consumers Association, www.organicconsumers.org.
• Myrna Chandler Goldstein and Mark Allan Goldstein, Controversies in Food and Nutrition (Greenwood Publishing Group, 2002), 13.

FACT: Blowfish (fugu), a delicacy in Japan and Hong Kong, contains deadly amounts oftetrodotoxin, a poison 500 times stronger than cyanide. Several diners die each year from blowfish consumption.

And yet, people continue to eat it. If I'm going to die from eating something, I assure you it won't be fish. Donuts, maybe, or bacon, but not fish.

• Dahlia Rideout, "Ten Dangerous & Deadly Foods," Divine Caroline,www.divinecaroline.com.
• Jack Jackson, Complete Diving Manual (New Holland Publishers,2005), 177.
• Robb Satterwhite, What's What in Japanese Restaurants: A Guide to Ordering, Eating, and Enjoying, 2nd ed. (Kodansha International,1996), 64.

F A C T : Because they are filter-feeders, shellfish can accumulate high levels of toxins from the algae they consume. Eat enough of them, and you could die.

Lobster and prawn: two more things I'd rather die from eating than blowfish.

• Dahlia Rideout, "Ten Dangerous & Deadly Foods," Divine Caroline, www.divinecaroline.com.
• "Various Shellfish-Associated Toxins," Bad Bug Book, U.S.Food and Drug Administration, Centre for Food Safety and Applied Nutrition, www.cfsan.fda.gov.

 F A C T : Rhubarb leaves contain a high concentration of oxalate, which is poisonous in large doses. The stems contain a lower concentration of oxalate, and also act as a good laxative.

Some foods were never meant for human consumption, and rhubarb is at the top of that list. The proof: it either poisons you or makes you crap yourself.

• Dahlia Rideout, "Ten Dangerous & Deadly Foods," Divine Caroline, www.divinecaroline.com.
• Ian Shaw, Is it Safe to Eat?: Enjoy Eating and Minimize Food Risks (Springer, 2005), 127.

 F A C T : Potatoes contain toxic compounds called glycoalkaloids that cannot be reduced in cooking. Consumption of high doses of glycoalkaloids can cause diarrhoea, vomiting, and, in severe cases, death.

Death by potato. Still better than death by blowfish.

• Dahlia Rideout, "Ten Dangerous & Deadly Foods," Divine Caroline, www.divinecaroline.com.
• Ian Shaw, Is it Safe to Eat?: Enjoy Eating and Minimize Food Risks (Springer, 2005), 127.

 F A C T : Apricot, cherry, and peach pits contain cyanogenetic glycosides, which release cyanide. It would take a huge dose to kill you, but there have been reports of children in Turkey suffering from apricot seed poisoning.

In case you needed another reason not to eat a peach pit. Imagine passing that thing.

• Dahlia Rideout, "Ten Dangerous & Deadly Foods," Divine Caroline, www.divinecaroline.com.
• Y.H. Hui, R. A. Smith, and David G. Spoerke, Plant Toxicants, 2nd ed. (Marcel Dekker,2001), 47.

 F A C T : Chocolate contains the alkaloid theobromine, which in high doses can be toxic to humans, and in even small amounts can kill dogs, parrots, horses, and cats.

This means that despite its name, the Kit-Kat bar is not a recommended snack for your kittycat. I wonder how many cats have died because of this confusion.

• Dahlia Rideout, "Ten Dangerous & Deadly Foods," Divine Caroline, www.divinecaroline.com.
• Lewis R. Goldfrank and others, Goldfrank's Toxicologic Emergencies, 8th ed. (McGraw-Hill Professional, 2006), 993.

 F A C T: If not processed properly, tapioca can be toxic; it is made from cassava root, which contains a natural cyanide-like compound called linamarin. If the plant is properly dried, soaked, and baked, however, the linamarin is rendered harmless and safe for consumption.

Soaked and Baked – two of my uni roommates.

• Dahlia Rideout, "Ten Dangerous & Deadly Foods," Divine Caroline, www.divinecaroline.com.
• Rudolph Ballentine, Diet &Nutrition: A Holistic Approach (Himalayan Institute Press,1982).

 F A C T: Bluefin tuna is popular at sushi bars, but it contains high amounts of mercury. Mercury poisoning can cause fatigue, memory loss, and numbness in extremities; recent studies also suggest that mercury can increase your risk of cardiovascular disease.

Do not confuse mercury poisoning with Freddie Mercury poisoning, which causes buck teeth, stage theatrics and an uncontrollable porn mustache.

• Aaron Casson Trenor, Sustainable Sushi: A Guide to Saving the Oceans One Bite at a Time (North Atlantic Books, 2009), 14.
• "High Mercury Levels Are Found in Tuna Sushi," New York Times, January 23, 2008, www.nytimes.com.

 F A C T: Though banned by all European nations and Canada, the synthetic hormone rBGH (Recombinant Bovine Growth Hormone) is still used by American dairy farmers to boost growth rates and increase body mass of cows, despite being linked to higher risks of breast cancer and hormonal disorders in humans who consume milk from those cows.

Got cancer?

• Samuel S. Epstein, Cancer-Gate: How to Win the Losing Cancer War (Baywood Publishing Company, 2005), 223.

F A C T: Over consumption of purine-rich foods like lobster, foie gras, and liver can lead to gout, a type of arthritis. Attacks can last for weeks, and can damage joints, tendons, and other tissues.

Gout has been called the 'rich man's disease' because of its association with fine foods like lobster and foie gras. But gout can also be caused by excessive alcohol use; this type is known as 'poor man's gout.' Those of us in the middle class are in the clear.

• "Gout – Topic Overview," Web Md, www.webmd.com.
• "Gout," The Free Dictionary Medical-Dictionary, http://medical-dictionary.thefreedictionary.com.
• "Gout," The-Family-Doctor.com, www.the-family-doctor.com.

F A C T: Campylobacter is a bacteria that can cause fever, diarrhoea, and abdominal cramps. Most raw poultry meat carries campylobacter, making consumption of undercooked chicken the main source for this infection.

Campylobacter does not commonly cause death. But consuming it will make you beg for death.

• "Campylobacter General Information," Centres for Disease Control and Prevention, Department of Health and Human Services, www.cdc.gov.

F A C T: E. coli O157:H7 is a bacterial pathogen found in cow faeces. Consuming water or food contaminated with even a tiny amount of bovine waste can lead to bloody diarrhoea, abdominal cramps, temporary anemia, and kidney failure.

Bloody diarrhoea: because neither bloody stool nor diarrhoea is enough fun on its own.

• "Food borne Illness," Content Source: National Centre for Immunization and Respiratory Diseases: Division of Bacterial Diseases, Centres for Disease Control and Prevention, Department of Health and Human Services, October 25, 2005,www.cdc.gov.

FACT: A century ago, the most common food borne diseases were typhoid fever, tuberculosis, and cholera. Today, we have a new list of food infections to worry about, including recent discoveries like cyclospora, a diarrhoea-causing parasite found in Guatemalan raspberries.

'Guatemalan raspberries' is also the nickname of this explosive type of diarrhoea. 'Start the game without me. I got the Guatemalan raspberries.'

• "Food borne Illness," Content Source: National Centre for Immunization and Respiratory Diseases: Division of Bacterial Diseases, Centres for Disease Control and Prevention, Department of Health and Human Services, October 25, 2005, www.cdc.gov.

THEY DID WHAT?!

Not-So-Proud Moments in World History

 F A C T: Ancient Romans used human urine as an ingredient in their toothpaste.

At least it wasn't pig urine. That would be disgusting.

• Joel Levy, Really Useful: The Origins of Everyday Things (Firefly Books, 2003).

 F A C T: Cruel treatment of slaves was forbidden in ancient Babylon by the Code of Hammurabi, but the code also commanded that slaves be branded on the forehead and forbidden to hide their mark.

That's why the Dress Code Of Hammurabi forbade headbands.

• Isaac Asimov, ed., Isaac Asimov's Book of Facts (Hastings House, 1979).

 F A C T: When a body was mummified in Ancient Egypt, the brain was removed through the nostrils, and other organs were stored in jars. Only the heart was left in the corpse.

I don't want to know how they got the other organs out. But I can guess. Hint: not through the nostrils.

• A. Lucas and John Richard Harris, Ancient Egyptian Materials and Industries, 4th ed. (Courier Dover Publications, 1999).

F A C T: A father in early Rome could legally sell any family member into slavery.

My dad would've loved early Rome.

• G. D. A. Sharpley, Essential Latin: The Language and Life of Ancient Rome, 2nd ed. (Routledge, 2000), 62.

F A C T: In early Rome, a father could legally execute any member of his household.

I'm glad I didn't grow up in early Rome.

• G. D. A. Sharpley, Essential Latin: The Language and Life of Ancient Rome, 2nd ed. (Routledge, 2000), 62.

F A C T: When blonde hair became fashionable in ancient Rome, thousands of Nordic blondes were captured or slain by Roman soldiers so that their hair could be used for wigs.

I guess this was before blondes started having more fun.

• Joanna Pitman, On Blondes (Bloomsbury, 2003), 26.

F A C T: In 336BC, King Philip II of Macedonia was murdered by a servant just as he was about to launch an invasion of Persia. Some historians suspect that the assassination was a conspiracy orchestrated by Philip's own son, Alexander The Great, so he could lead the Macedonians to victory instead of his father.

And so he could change his name from 'Alexander The Just Average,' which was given to him by his father.

• Thom Burnett, Conspiracy Encyclopedia: The Encyclopedia of Conspiracy Theories (Franz Steiner Verlag, 2006).

F A C T: Ancient Egyptian court records dating to 1500BC include the world's oldest recorded death sentence. A teenage male convicted of 'magic' was ordered to kill himself by either poison or stabbing.

Magicians should be killed. Jugglers and mimes, too. And clowns for sure.

• Charles Panati, Panati's Extraordinary Endings of Practically Everything and Everybody (New York: Harper & Row, 1989).

F A C T: The Classic Mayan civilization thrived for over 600 years before collapsing abruptly in the ninth century. The cause of their extinction is unknown, and still debated today, more than 1,100 years later.

By nerds with nothing better to do.

• Frank Joseph, ed., Unearthing Ancient America: The Lost Sagas of Conquerors, Castaways, and Scoundrels (Franklin Lakes, NJ: New Page Books, 2009).

 F A C T: Poor Aztec peasants picked lice from their bodies and offered that to the king when they had no gold to give.

Even the Aztecs knew that gifts that you make are so much more thoughtful than others.

• Bruce Felton and Mark Fowler, Felton & Fowler's More Best, Worst, and Most Unusual (New York: Thomas Y. Crowell Company, 1976).

 F A C T: Every day, Martin Luther ate a spoonful of his own excrement. He wrote praises to God for his generosity in giving man such an important and useful remedy.

CUT TO: God, laughing His arse off.

• Rose George, The Big Necessity: The Unmentionable World of Human Waste and Why It Matters (St. Martin's Press, 2008).

 F A C T: Vikings sent eighty 'dragon ships' outfitted with 100 soldiers each, in a single raid on Britain around the year 1000. The King of England usually asked for a red shirt when he saw an enemy ship approaching, so that if he was wounded in battle and bled, his men would not notice.

When he saw the eighty Vikings ships coming, however, the King asked for his brown trousers.

• Isaac Asimov, ed., Isaac Asimov's Book of Facts (Hastings House, 1979).

 F A C T: In 1014, the original London Bridge was destroyed by Saxons, who rowed warships up the river Thames, attached cables to the bridge, and pulled it down as they rowed away.

It took awhile. They started pulling in 1012.

• Jack Mingo and Erin Barrett, Just Curious, Jeeves: What Are the 1001 Most Intriguing Questions Asked on the Internet? (Emeryville, CA: Ask Jeeves Inc., 2000).

 F A C T: During the bloody thirty-eight year reign of Henry VIII (1509–1547), an estimated 57,000 to 72,000 subjects lost their heads.

They never found them, either.

• Julia Layton, "Top 10 Heads That Rolled During the Reign of Henry VIII," HowStuffWorks.com, www.howstuffworks.com.

 F A C T: In 1517, Spanish missionary Bartolomé de Las Casas, disgusted by the enslavement of Native Americans by Spanish colonizers, suggested bringing Africans to the New World as slaves instead. De Las Casas also suggested that Spain start its own Inquisition and send its Armada to invade England.

Then they shot him before he could make any other suggestions.

• David Wallechinsky and Irving Wallace, The People's Almanac #2 (New York: Bantam Books, 1978).

 F A C T: In the process of divorcing Catherine of Aragon and marrying Anne Boleyn, his mistress, Henry VIII ordered the beheadings of many who questioned his motives, including political leaders, high-ranking church officials, two of his six wives, and countless members of his royal court.

Wouldn't it have been funny if all the lopped-off heads woke up and started right back to slagging off Henry about his divorce.

• Julia Layton, "Top 10 Heads That Rolled During the Reign of Henry VIII," HowStuffWorks.com, www.howstuffworks.com.

 F A C T: St Edmund the Martyr, King of East Anglia, was killed by the Vikings in 869 after they defeated his army. According to legend, Edmund's executioners either 'spread-eagled' him, prying open his ribs and exposing his still-breathing lungs, or whipped him, shot him with arrows, and eventually chopped off his head.

'Hmm,' said Edmund, upon hearing his choices, 'is there by chance a third option?'

- Ian Crofton, Brewer's Cabinet of Curiosities (Cassell, 2006).
- "St. Edmund The Martyr," Catholic Encyclopedia, www.newadvent.org.

F A C T: After victory in battle, Vikings drank the blood of vanquished enemies from human skulls, hence the Scandinavian toast, 'Skol!'

Is there really any other way to drink blood?

- Bruce Felton and Mark Fowler, Felton & Fowler's More Best, Worst, and Most Unusual (New York: Thomas Y. Crowell Company, 1976).

F A C T: Pope John XII was deposed by Roman Emperor Otto I in 963 for raping female pilgrims to St Peter's, stealing church offerings, drinking toasts to the devil, and invoking the aid of pagan gods. John XII reportedly died from a stroke while in bed with a married woman.

Pope John XII: 'What?! You're firing me? What'd I do?' That's what fired people always say. Like it's a surprise.

- Simon Adams and Lesley Riley, eds., Reader's Digest Facts & Fallacies (Pleasantville, NY: Reader's Digest Association 1988).
- Eamon Duffy, Saints & Sinners: A History of the Popes, 3rd ed. (Yale University Press, 2006).

F A C T: When red precipitation fell on Paris on Easter Sunday in 582, terrified people believed that it was raining blood, a sign of divine displeasure. Theories suggest that the 'rain' was red sand particles stirred by strong windstorms in the Sahara and blown across the Mediterranean Sea into Europe.

At least it wasn't raining men. That would have been worse.

- Randy Cerveny, Freaks of the Storm: From Flying Cows to Ste

F A C T: In 1732, King George II gave General James Oglethorpe a charter to create a new colony in America, where imprisoned British debtors could be relocated so that they might start new lives and become self-sufficient.

That colony became the state of Georgia. They should've stayed in prison.

• Alexander Hewatt, An Historical Account of the Rise and Progress of the Colonies of South Carolina and Georgia (Biblio Bazaar, 2007), 24.

 F A C T: The Indian removal put in place by President Andrew Jackson forced the Cherokee nation to vacate the southern U.S. and move west to what is now Oklahoma. Their long journey in 1838–1839 was dubbed the 'Trail Of Tears' after it claimed the lives of 4,000 Cherokee – almost a third of their population – from hunger, disease, and exhaustion.

I'd rather die than live in Oklahoma, too.

• "Indian removal," PBS.org,www.pbs.org.
• "The Trail of Tears," PBS.org, www.pbs.org.

 F A C T: In May 1902, volcanic activity on the Caribbean island of Martinique drove more than a hundred fer-de-lance snakes into the town of St Pierre, where the large, venomous reptiles killed fifty people and hundreds of animals.

Fer-de-love of God, do they not have cats on that island?

• David Wallechinsky, The New Book of Lists: The Original Compendium of Curious Information (Canon gate U.S., 2005).

 F A C T: India tested its first nuclear bomb in 1974.

Indian food sets off a few bombs of its own.

• "Nuclear Proliferation," U.S. Department Of Energy, Office Of History & Heritage, www.doe.gov.

 F A C T: From 1915 to 1918, 2 million Armenians were slaughtered or deported from their historic Asia Minor homeland by the Turkish government, which also demolished ancient cities, architecture, and records, removing nearly all traces of the 3,000-year-old civilization.

'Would you like to be slaughtered or deported?' 'Hmm, let me think. I think I'll go with deported.'

• "Armenian Genocide," The Armenian Genocide Museum-Institute, www.genocide-museum.am.

FACT: An estimated 7 million people died during the Ukraine famine of 1932–1933, about 25,000 a day at its peak. The famine was engineered by Joseph Stalin to destroy the region's drive for independence.

• "Ukrainian Genocide of 1932–1933," Ukrainian Genocide Famine Foundation-USA, Inc., www.ukrainiangenocide.com.
• "Ukranian Famine," Ibiblio.org, www.ibiblio.org.

FACT: By the end of World War II, nearly all of Europe's Jewish population had been wiped out by the Holocaust: 4 million in Adolf Hitler's death camps, and 2 million in ghettos in Warsaw, Theresienstadt, and other cities.

• "The Holocaust," United States Holocaust Memorial Museum, www.ushmm.org.

FACT: China's Chairman Mao Zedong was a ruthless leader whose policies wiped out millions of Chinese. In the 1950s, Mao's so-called 'Great Leap Forward' of collective farming and rapid industrialization led to famine throughout China, killing as many as 35 million people.

• "1976: Chairman Mao Dies," On This Day, BBC News, http://news.bbc.co.uk.

FACT: China's Cultural Revolution, started by Chairman Mao Zedong in 1966 to purge opponents, dragged on for 10 years and slaughtered tens of thousands of Chinese citizens.

And that concludes this episode of 'History's Biggest arse holes.'

• "China's Communist Revolution: A Glossary," BBC News, http://news.bbc.co.uk.

FACT: Fourteen years before the *Titanic* sank, a novel titled *Futility* told the story of an ocean liner named Titan that met its demise one April night when it collided with an iceberg.

A novel that didn't sell a lot of copies, I'm guessing.

• Facts Library, www.factlib.com.

FACT: In July 1945, a B-25 crashed into the Empire State Building in New York, engulfing six floors in flames. Amazingly, only 14 people died: the crash happened on a Saturday and the building was all but empty.

Hopefully they were stockbrokers.

• David Wallechinsky, The New Book of Lists: The Original Compendium of Curious Information (Canongate U.S., 2005), 397.

 F A C T: Since the 1950s, several of the most notorious dictators, mass murderers, and state terrorists of Latin America have trained at the Western Hemisphere Institute for Security Cooperation (formerly the School of the Americas) run by the CIA at Fort Benning, Georgia.

Yes, but they pay out-of-state tuition, and they need the money.

• Thom Burnett, Conspiracy Encyclopedia: The Encyclopedia of Conspiracy Theories (Franz Steiner Verlag, 2006),

 F A C T: In 1981, President Ronald Reagan approved nutrition guidelines that qualified ketchup as a vegetable in school lunches, saving the U.S. government millions of dollars.

That's preposterous. Everyone knows the tomato is a fruit, not a vegetable.

• Susan Levine, School Lunch Politics: The Surprising History of America's Favourite Welfare Program (Princeton University Press, 2008), 177.

 F A C T: One week prior to his assassination, President Abraham Lincoln had a dream about someone crying in the White House. He followed the sound to a room where he found a man by a coffin. When Lincoln asked who had died, the man replied, 'The President.'

But the man by the coffin was Bill Clinton, so Lincoln didn't believe him.

• "Facts About Abraham Lincoln," Abraham Lincoln Library, www.alincoln-library.com.

 F A C T: Napoleon used a sandbox to construct his battle plans.

He was too short to reach the map tables.

• Facts Library, www.factlib.com.

I FOUGHT THE LAW AND THE LAW WON

LAW AND ORDER IN THE WORLD AND WORKPLACE

 FACT: The United States has 2.3 million people behind bars, making it the world leader in the number and percentage of residents they incarcerate. China is a distant second.

That's because China just executes its criminals instead.

• "New High In U.S. Prison Numbers," Washington Post, February 29, 2008, www.washingtonpost.com.

 FACT: Two-thirds of the world's executions occur in China.

Told you. Two-thirds in China, one-third in Texas.

• Tania Branigan, "China Proclaims Big Fall in Executions after Court Reforms," The Guardian, March 11, 2006, www.guardian.co.uk.

 FACT: In 1986, Wisconsinite Stephen Avery was convicted for sexual assault, attempted murder, and false imprisonment, but was exonerated eighteen years later by DNA evidence. In 2007, just four years out of prison, Avery was convicted again, this time for the murder of a young woman, and sentenced to life in prison.

And they say you can't go home again.

• Russ Kick, Disinformation Book of Lists: Subversive Facts and Hidden Information in Rapidfire

Format [The Disinformation Company, 2004].
• "The Murder of Teresa Halbach," TruTV, www.trutv.com.

F A C T: It took two jolts of electricity to kill murderer Frank J. Coppola when he was executed by electrocution in 1982, the second of which caused Coppola's head and leg to catch fire. A spectator later reported that the odour of burning flesh and smoke had filled the death chamber.

Replacing the usual delightful aroma of the death chamber.

• Russ Kick, Disinformation Book of Lists: Subversive Facts and Hidden Information in Rapid-fire Format [The Disinformation Company, 2004].

F A C T: When Jimmy Lee Gray was executed by asphyxiation in 1983 for murdering a three-year old girl, his gasps for air were so desperate that authorities cleared the room of witnesses. Gray's lawyer said, 'Gray died banging his head against a steel pole in the gas chamber while reporters counted his moans.' His executioner was later revealed to have been drunk at the time.

Karma's a bitch, ain't it?

• Russ Kick, Disinformation Book of Lists: Subversive Facts and Hidden Information in Rapidfire Format [The Disinformation Company, 2004].

F A C T: During the execution of serial killer John Wayne Gacy in 1994 in Illinois, the lethal serum solidified and got clogged up in the IV tube leading to Gacy's arm. Executioners had to start again, and the process took eighteen minutes to complete.

And this was before smart phones, so it's not like you could text anyone or check your e-mail while waiting for them to finish him.

• Russ Kick, Disinformation Book of Lists: Subversive Facts and Hidden Information in Rapidfire Format [The Disinformation Company, 2004].

F A C T: When Allen Lee Davis was executed in Florida in 1999 for beating to death a pregnant woman and her two young daughters, blood spewed from his mouth and he suffered burns to his head, leg, and groin. This marked the debut of the state's new electric chair, built specifically to accommodate a man OF Davis' size (25 stones).

Hopefully it had wheels.

• Russ Kick, Disinformation Book of Lists: Subversive Facts and Hidden Information in Rapidfire Format (The Disinformation Company, 2004).

 F A C T: Approximately 25 per cent of wrongful convictions are made because of incriminating statements and false confessions. In more than a third of these, defendants were developmentally disabled and under the age of eighteen.

Remember, kids: if you must make an incriminating statement, just be sure it incriminates someone else.

• "Facts on Post-Conviction DNA Exonerations," Innocence Project, www.innocenceproject.org.

 F A C T: According to Amnesty International, security forces in southern Thai provinces engage in systematic torture and abuse during regional conflicts. Prisoners are beaten, burned, buried in the ground up to their necks, given electric shocks, and nearly suffocated with plastic bags, leading to several deaths.

Human rights abuses in southeast Asia? Nooooo!

• "Thai Security Forces Systematically Torture in Southern Counter-Insurgency," Amnesty International, January 13, 2009, www.amnesty.org.

 F A C T: A police officer in Florida shocked an eleven-year-old child with a learning disability with a Taser when she punched him. The school called the police after the child became agitated and assaulted staff.

They just need a lower setting on that thing, one for children, animals, midgets, and the elderly.

• "Tasers – Potentially Lethal and Easy to Abuse," Amnesty International, December 16 2008, www.amnesty.org.

 F A C T: Hanging originated about 2,500 years ago in Persia as a method of execution. It became the favoured method in many countries because it remained a visible deterrent to crime but was less gory than beheading.

You might know Persia better as modern-day Iran, and, if you do, you can't be too surprised that they invented hanging.

• "Hanged by the neck until dead," Capital Punishment U.K., www.capitalpunishmentuk.org.

 F A C T: Crucifixion was the most common form of execution in ancient Rome, but today it is an official method of capital punishment in just one country: Sudan.

Modern-day crucifixion – from the fine people who brought you Darfur.

• Tom Head, "Death by Crucifixion: An Overview and History of Death by Crucifixion," About.com, www.about.com.
• Donald G. Kyle, Spectacles of Death in Ancient Rome (Routledge, 2001).
• "Sudan: Imminent Execution/Torture/Unfair Trial," Amnesty International, www.amnesty.org.

 F A C T: Charles Taylor, one of West Africa's most bloodthirsty warlords, drugged his legions of child soldiers, called 'Small Boy Units,' with cocktails of cocaine, gunpowder, and amphetamines. He has been defending himself in a court in The Hague, Netherlands against charges of killings, mutilations, rape, and sexual slavery.

They should try him in Iran. They invented hanging, you know.

• "Spider Men," Crimes and Punishments, Lapham's Quarterly, Spring 2009.

 F A C T: Yakuza, the Japanese mafia, consider themselves descendents of samurai. The gangsters dress kidnapped women in short, pleated skirts and knee-high socks to cater for a 'school girl' sex market. They also sell unwanted Chinese boys on the black market.

They also cut off Andy Garcia's head in Black Rain. I realise that it was just a film, but come on, that was just uncalled for.

• "Spider Men," Crimes and Punishments, Lapham's Quarterly, Spring 2009.

 F A C T: Pirate attacks off the Horn of Africa tripled in 2008. Somali pirates assaulted more than a hundred ships and captured at least forty, extorting up to $150 million in ransom from ship owners around the world. Among crafts hijacked: a Ukrainian freighter carrying thirty-three Soviet tanks, and a supertanker delivering $100million in Saudi crude oil.

Worse, they always demand the ransom in gold doubloons and barrels of rum, which are hard to find nowadays.

• Matthew Power, "Hostile Takeovers," Crimes and Punishments, Lapham's Quarterly, Spring 2009.

 F A C T: In 1991, Milwaukee police officers, responding to a 911 call, found a naked teenage boy attempting to flee from a man. The soft-spoken thirty-year-old man explained to the police that he and the boy were merely lovers having a domestic dispute. The man was so polite and persuasive that the police let him take the boy back to his apartment, where the man, serial killer Jeffrey Dahmer, strangled the boy, had sex with his body, and dismembered him. Dahmer was arrested two months later and convicted of fifteen murders. He was killed by another inmate in prison in 1994.

Most people remember exactly where they were and what they were doing when they heard the news that Jeffrey Dahmer had been killed. Wait – no, I'm thinking of JFK. Never mind.

• Harold Schechter and David Everitt, The A to Z Encyclopedia of Serial Killers (Simon & Schuster, 2006).

 F A C T: Dr Henry Howard Holmes was America's first serial killer. Holmes built a Chicago mansion complete with trap doors, secret passageways, and rooms lined with asbestos that could be turned into gas chambers. Upon his capture in 1894, Holmes confessed to twenty-seven murders. He was hanged in 1896.

Holmes wouldn't confess to more of his murders because he didn't want people to think he was an animal.

• "World's worst killers," BBC News, October 30, 1999, www.news.bbc.co.uk.
• Harold Schechter and David Everitt, The A to Z Encyclopedia of Serial Killers (Simon & Schuster, 2006).

 F A C T: In 1989, Erik and Lyle Menendez were charged with the murder of their wealthy parents. The boys were not considered suspects until six months after their parents' death, when their lavish spending caught investigators' attention. The Menendez brothers were convicted and sentenced in 1996 to life in prison without parole.

They were also given a copy of Lying Low For Dummies.

• S. L. Alexander, Media and American Courts: A Reference Handbook (ABC-CLIO, 2004).

 F A C T: Richard Kuklinski was known as a diabolical contract killer. He committed his first murder at age fourteen, and later became a mob hitman, using weapons like cyanide and chainsaws to commit brutal murders. Kuklinski was nicknamed Iceman because he sometimes froze corpses to disguise the time of death.

At least he was doing something he enjoyed. They say that's important.

• Charles Montaldo, "Profile of Richard Kuklinski: The Iceman,"About.com: Crime/Punishment, www.crime.about.com.
• Douglas Martin, "Richard Kuklinski, 70, a Killer of Many People and Many Ways, Dies," New York Times, March 9, 2006.

 F A C T: By law, all citizens must take a bath at least once a year in Kentucky.

Whether they need it or not.

• "Ky Law Mandates Bathing Once A Year," redOrbit.com, November 23, 2003, www.redorbit.com.

 F A C T: Two Domino's Pizza employees were arrested in 2009 after a video surfaced on the Internet that showed one of them putting cheese up his nose while preparing sandwiches, farting on salami slices, and blowing his nose on the food, as the second employee filmed it and boasted about giving the tainted food to customers.

Farting on salami seems a little redundant.

• "Domino's Prankster A Sex Offender," The Smoking Gun, April 16, 2009, www.thesmokinggun.com.

 F A C T: It is illegal to get a fish intoxicated in the state of Ohio.

And not really necessary if you buy it a nice dinner and sweet-talk it a little.

• Alex Wade, "The World's Strangest Laws," Times Online, August 15, 2007, www.business. timesonline.co.uk.

FACT: It is illegal for unmarried women to parachute in Florida on Sundays; violators can be arrested.

As they should be. From that altitude, Florida looks like a giant penis, and no unmarried woman should be looking at that, especially on the Lord's day.

• Alex Wade, "The World's Strangest Laws," Times Online, August 15, 2007, www.business. timesonline.co.uk.

FACT: You should never carry concealed weapons longer than six feet in the state of Kentucky – the offense is punishable by law.

Is that a howitzer in your trousers or are you just pleased to see me?

• Alex Wade, "The World's Strangest Laws," Times Online, August 15, 2007, www.business. timesonline.co.uk.

FACT: It is illegal to own pets in Boulder, Colorado – locals are considered 'pet minders' only. It is also illegal to kill a bird.

Two good laws, because anyone who owns a bird usually wants to kill it after a day or two.

• Alex Wade, "The World's Strangest Laws," Times Online, August 15, 2007, www.business. timesonline.co.uk.

FACT: Vermont women must get written permission from their husbands before they get false teeth.

Some men prefer their women toothless, if you know what I mean (wink wink).

• Alex Wade, "The World's Strangest Laws," Times Online, August 15, 2007, www.business. timesonline.co.uk.

FACT: The Brady Bill and Assault Weapons Ban were enacted in 1993. In the five years that followed, nine school shooting massacres occurred.

I guess the 'ban' is still a work in progress.

• "Gun Control," Just Facts, www.justfacts.com.

 F A C T: In August 1986, U.S. Postal Service worker Patrick Henry Sherrill – or 'Crazy Pat,' as he was called – shot and killed 14 colleagues in the Edmond, Oklahoma post office where he was employed, including a supervisor who had criticized his work.

Hmm, I wonder why they called him 'Crazy Pat.'

• Jacob V. Lamar Jr., "'Crazy Pat's' Revenge," Time, June 24, 2001, www.time.com.
• Charles Montaldo, "It's Official:' Going Postal' Is Epidemic," About.com, www.about.com.

 F A C T: In 1976, the typical CEO earned thirty-six times the salary of his average worker. Today, the average CEO makes 369 times what an average worker makes.

Both of them are unemployed now, and 369 times zero is zero.

• Steven Greenhouse, The Big Squeeze: Tough Times for the American Worker (Random House, 2008).

 F A C T: In a 2004 survey, 17 per cent of men said they had been sexually harassed on the job, but 60 per cent of them did nothing about it.

Those 60 per cent are the ones who liked it.

• "Interoffice Romance Survey," Lawyers.com, August 12, 2004, www.research.lawyers.com.
• "Sexual Harassment In The Workplace," Sexual Harassment Support, www.sexualharassmentsupport.org.

 F A C T: Claims of karoshi – death by overwork – jumped after Japan modified a rule to include the effects of cumulative fatigue. A worker who dies after routinely working eighty or more overtime hours a month is now eligible to be considered a case of karoshi.

If I had to work eighty or more overtime hours a month, I would welcome death.

• Rory O'Neill, "Drop Dead," Hazards Magazine, July–September 2003, www.hazards.org.

F A C T: A study published in 2002 concludes that workers who perform meaningless work with minimal chance for input were at higher risk of dying young.

In other words, everyone but CEO.

• Rory O'Neill, "Drop Dead," Hazards Magazine, July–September 2003, www.hazards.org.

F A C T: In 2003, 1,400 government employees in India committed suicide or died from starvation. They had not been paid in more than a decade. The state officials responsible were charged with theft, reportedly using employee funds for lavish foreign trips.

So impatient. They couldn't wait one more day for payday?

• Agence France-Presse, "World Briefing | Asia: India: Inquiry Into Deaths Of Government Workers," New York Times, November 14, 2003, www.nytimes.com.

F A C T: In a 2004 poll, 12 per cent of respondents confessed to having sex in the workplace, while another 10 per cent said they fantasised about it.

Jack and Sarah often worked late, leveraging each other's assets and pumping up the bottom line.

• "Poll: American Sex Survey: A Peek Beneath The Sheets," ABC News, October 21, 2004, http://abcnews.go.com.

F A C T: Researchers concluded in 2008 that bullying at work, such as persistent criticism of work, belittling comments, and withholding resources, is more harmful to employees than sexual harassment.

Belittling comments, persistent criticism and withholding 'resources'? Sounds more like marriage than the workplace.

• M. Sandy Hershcovis and Julian Barling, "Bullying More Harmful Than Sexual Harassment On The Job, Say Researchers," Science Daily, March 9, 2008, www.sciencedaily.com.

F A C T: Workplace bullying affects 25 to 30 per cent of employees at some time during their careers.

Instead of lunch money, they take your parking spot.

• Jeanna Bryner, "Strange News, Study: Office Bullies Create Workplace 'Warzone'," Live Science, October 31, 2006, www.livescience.com.

F A C T: In March 2009, a Louisiana high-school teacher was arrested for obscenity after three students and another teacher witnessed him masturbating in a classroom.

I guess he hadn't heard: spanking in schools was outlawed years ago.

• "Higgins Teacher Arrested For Obscenity," WWLTV.com, March 20, 2009, www.wwltv.com.

F A C T: One out of three companies that go bankrupt each year do so as a result of employee theft. Almost 80 per cent of workers admit that they have, or would consider, stealing from their employers.

If a few filched Post-It Notes and paper clips can drive a company out of business, they probably weren't going to last long, anyway.

• Nicole Jacoby, "Battling Workplace Theft," CNN Money, August 19, 1999, www.money.cnn.com.

F A C T: A woman claims that she was fired from her job in 2007 for chronic flatulence. The unnamed woman, who suffers from irritable bowel syndrome, says she was frequently harassed and taunted about her problem by colleagues before being terminated.

That really stinks. What a bunch of arses. There's a happy ending, though: she found work at the gas company.

• Lucy Thornton, "Woman Fired Over Farting Claims," Mirror.co.uk, May 12, 2007, www.mirror.co.uk

F A C T: Eight of every ten e-mails sent worldwide are spam. American companies lose an estimated $22 billion annually in time spent deleting junk e-mail.

The other two of ten are hoaxes, chain mail, urban myths, and other crap with little flashing hearts and teddy bears, sent by your mum.

• Swartz, Nikki, "Deleting Spam Costs Businesses Billions," Information Management Journal, May/Jun 2005, www.findarticles.com

The X-Files

Facts and Claims about Aliens, Ghosts, Jedward, and Other Realms of the Unexplained

F A C T: U.S. citizens are not legally permitted to come into contact with extraterrestrials or their vehicles, according to Title 14, section 1211 of the Code of Federal Regulations, implemented in 1969.

Does that include sex? What if you weren't aware of the law at the time?

• Mary Bennett and David Percy, *Dark Moon: Apollo and the Whistle-Blowers* (Adventures Unlimited Press, 2001).

F A C T: In July 1947, the U.S. Army Air Forces announced that they had recovered a flying saucer that crashed near Roswell Air Army Field in New Mexico. Within hours, however, the Army dismissed the statement, claiming that the flying saucer was a misidentified weather balloon.

• Thomas J. Carey, Donald R. Schmitt, *Witness to Roswell: Unmasking the 60-Year Cover-Up* (Career Press, 2007), 27–29.

F A C T: Since 1947, the U.S. government has changed its explanation of the Roswell crash four times. It remains one of the most a controversial, highly publicised UFO incidents in history.

At least among the sixty-seven people who actually believe that shit.

• Thomas J. Carey, Donald R. Schmitt, Witness to Roswell: Unmasking the 60-Year Cover-Up (Career Press, 2007), 27–29.

 F A C T: Pine Bush, New York is known as the UFO capital of the East Coast, as many residents believe that extraterrestrials have been frequenting their town for the last decade. A support group was founded there in 1993 for locals who believe that they've had encounters with these aliens.

'Hi, my name's Leo and I'm an alien shagger.' (Group): 'Hi, Leo.'

• Chris Gethard, Mark Moran, and Mark Sceurman, Weird New York: Your Travel Guide to New York's Local Legends and Best Kept Secrets (Sterling Publishing Company, 2005).

 F A C T: The Tower of London is said to be full of ghosts, including that of the Countess of Salisbury, who, according to legend, was hacked to death by her pursuing executioner as she tried to escape. Some claim that spirits reenact the grisly 16th century event on Tower Green.

If any place in the world has ghosts, the Tower of London is it.

• Lionel Fanthorpe and Patricia Fanthorpe, The World's Most Mysterious Castles (DundurnPress Ltd., 2005), 184.

 F A C T: On February 11, 1859, thousands of small fish rained over the village of Mountain Ash in South Wales, one of several recorded instances of live fish falling from the sky.

Live until they hit the ground, that is.

• John Michell, Bob Rickard, and Robert J. M. Rickard, Unexplained Phenomena: A Rough Guide Special (Rough Guides, 2000), 18.
• Susan Cosier, "It's Raining Fish," Science Line, September 17, 2006, www.scienceline.org.

 F A C T: The Bermuda Triangle and the Oregon Vortex are believed by some to be connected to 'magnetic vortexes,' in which the walls between known and unknown dimensions are so thin that people can pass through them and seemingly disappear.

Some people believe in the Tooth Fairy, too.

• Nicholas R. Nelson, Paradox: A Round Trip Through the Bermuda Triangle (New Horizon, 1980).

F A C T: In 1891, a sailor aboard the whaling ship *The Star of the East* disappeared while trying to kill a great sperm whale. After the whale was caught and its stomach cut open, the ship's crew found the missing sailor curled up inside but still alive.

He was rocking back and forth, whimpering, and sucking his thumb.

• Stephen Wagner, "Seven of the Weirdest Human Enigmas," About.com, www.paranormal.about.com.

F A C T: In 1962, a poltergeist harassed an Indianapolis grandmother, mother, and daughter by making noises, hurling objects, and biting them. The initial string of incidents stopped after two weeks, but the poltergeist would return several times over the following months.

Poltergeists are German, so they're very stubborn and not easily deterred.

• James Houran and Rense Lange, Hauntings and Poltergeists: Multidisciplinary Perspectives (McFarland, 2001), 65.

F A C T: From 1920 to 1950, the Glastenbury Mountains area of Vermont saw several disappearances, including a student who vanished while walking in the woods, a man who disappeared from a bus, and a child who went missing from his family's farm. The region has since become known as 'The Bennington Triangle.'

Bus man probably died in the toilet and is still there. No one would notice the smell.

• Joseph A. Citro, Weird New England: Your Travel Guide to New England's Local Legends and Best Kept Secrets (Sterling Publishing Company, 2005), 75.

F A C T: In 1913, satirist Ambrose Bierce disappeared in Mexico after travelling there to witness Pancho Villa's revolution. Scholars believe that the seventy-one-year-old man was killed in the siege of Ojinaga, while others speculate that Bierce's final letters were a ruse and that he never actually went to Mexico, but instead committed suicide.

Maybe he went for a walk in the Glastenbury Mountains in Vermont.

• Joe Nickell, Unsolved History: Investigating Mysteries of the Past (University Press of Kentucky, 2005).

 F A C T: During her 1937 attempt to fly around the world, pioneering female pilot Amelia Earhart disappeared over the Pacific Ocean. Military ships scoured a wide area for any sign of Earhart, her co-pilot, or the plane, but none was ever found.

Did she fly over Vermont?

• "Top Ten Famous Disappearances," Time.com, www.time.com.

 F A C T: On June 11, 1962, inmates Frank Morris and Clarence and John Anglin escaped from Alcatraz prison during the night. Despite one of the largest manhunts since the Lindbergh kidnapping, the trio were never found.

Oh, they were found. By sharks. After they drowned.

• "Top Ten Famous Disappearances," Time.com, www.time.com.

 F A C T: After James Dean was killed in a 1955 car accident, remnant parts of his Porsche Spyder were said to be cursed. Subsequent owners of those parts allegedly suffered numerous injuries and at least one was killed. Following a 1960 exhibition in Miami, the wreckage of the cursed car disappeared while en route to Los Angeles.

Did the route go through Vermont, by any chance?

• Tom Ogden, The Complete Idiot's Guide to Ghosts and phantoms (Alpha Books, 1999), 251.

 F A C T: George Herbert, one of the men who found the tomb of King Tutankhamen in 1922, died from tuberculosis and blood poisoning shortly after, and Cairo is said to have experienced a city-wide power outage at the time of Herbert's death. Both events are blamed on the 'Curse of the Pharoah.'

According to legend, the curse stems from the fact that Tut was buried in his pyjamas, something the ancient king would not have wanted made public.

• S. T. Joshi, Icons of Horror and the Supernatural: An Encyclopedia of Our Worst Nightmares (Greenwood Publishing Group, 2007).

F A C T: Since the 1991 discovery of the Ice Man, several people connected to the research of the 5,000-year-old specimen have met their death, giving him his own version of 'The Curse of Tutankhamen.'

Similarly, the discovery of Vanilla Ice in the early 1990s has led to the deaths of several hundred people, all by their own hand.

• Brian Haughton, Hidden History: Lost Civilizations, Secret Knowledge, and Ancient Mysteries (Career Press, 2007).

F A C T: A creature called Spring-Heeled Jack terrorised London residents in the nineteenth century. The orange-eyed beast scratched victims in the face and body, then leapt away with inhuman ability.

The police put Scooby-Doo and the gang on the case. They exposed the 'monster' as a local prospector trying to scare away residents. And he would've gotten away with it, too, if it hadn't been for those meddling kids.

• Matt Lake and Mark Moran, Weird England: Your Travel Guide to England's Local Legends and Best Kept Secrets (Sterling Publishing Company, 2007), 59.

F A C T: In 1996, rural villagers in Puerto Rico reported a rash of strange deaths among goats, whose bodies were found completely drained of blood, with puncture wounds on their necks. Locals blamed the Chupacabra, or 'goat sucker,' for the still unexplained incidents.

Such fanciful attributions are typical among the uneducated. More astute observers recognised these events for what they were: the work of vampires.

• Robert Todd Carroll, The Skeptic's Dictionary: A Collection of Strange Beliefs, Amusing Deceptions, and Dangerous Delusions (John Wiley & Sons, 2003), 76.

F A C T: The Moehau, New Zealand's version of Bigfoot, is said to stab victims with a long, bony finger.

At least they hope that's a finger.

• Jonathan Maberry and David F. Kramer, The Cryptopedia: A Dictionary of the Weird, Strange & Downright Bizarre (Kensington Publishing, 2007), 30.

F A C T: In 1924, a group of miners in Washington's Mount Saint Helens range were reportedly attacked by eight-foot tall 'Bigfoot' humanoids, who knocked on the doors, walls, and roof of their cabin.

Or maybe they were just attacked by a bad batch of moonshine.

• Colin Wilson and Damon Wilson, The Mammoth Encyclopedia of the Unsolved (Carroll & Graf, 2000).

 F A C T: In 1856, a pterodactyl was discovered in France by workers blasting rocks to build a railway. The beast used its ten-foot wingspan to stagger out into the sunlight before it let out a hoarse cry and died. Naturalists identified the creature and the rock strata as being millions of years old.

The hoarse cry was pterodactyl for, 'Christ, not France.'

• David Hatcher Childress, Lost Cities & Ancient Mysteries of Africa & Arabia (Adventures Unlimited Press, 1989).

 F A C T: South Americans are terrorised by minhocão, a giant worm beleived to be seventy feet long with armour-plated skin, a pig-like snout, and two tentacles on its head. Spotted in Uruguay and southern Brazil, the minhocão lives underground but occasionally surfaces, and many blame it for collapsed bridges, tunnels, and roadways.

Others know a train when they see it and are not afraid.

• Jonathan Maberry and David F. Kramer, The Cryptopedia: A Dictionary of the Weird, Strange & Downright Bizarre (Kensington Publishing, 2007), 30.

 F A C T: Zambia is home to Pterodactyl-like flying monsters called kongamato, which are said to have bat-like wings with four- to seven-foot spans and a long, tapered jaw filled with sharp teeth.

Zambian villagers believe that to look upon the kongamato is death. Others know a hang-glider when they see it and are not afraid.

• David Hatcher Childress, Lost Cities & Ancient Mysteries of Africa & Arabia (Adventures Unlimited Press, 1989).

F A C T: Scientists are unable to explain a number of fossils that have been found, including one of a human handprint in limestone and a human finger found in the Arctic in Canada, both estimated to be 100–110 million years old.

I'm unable to explain the number of fossils driving cars around my village; I thought being able to see over the steering wheel – or at all – was required for a driver's license.

• Stephen Wagner, "Impossible Fossils," About.com, www.paranormal.about.com.

 F A C T: In 1938, an archeological expedition in China discovered hundreds of stone disks in caves in the Baian-Kara-Ula mountains, each measuring nine inches in diameter and etched with miniscule hieroglyphics that tell a story of aircrafts from distant worlds crashing in the mountains. The disks are believed to be thousands of years old.

And a possible indication of when man discovered opium.

• Stephen Wagner, "Impossible Fossils," About.com, www.paranormal.about.com.

 F A C T: Crystal skulls found in Mexico have long fascinated archaeologists. One specimen, sold at Sotheby's in 1943, is known as the 'Skull of Doom' and is said to have mystical powers, emit blue lights from its eyes, and crash computer hard drives.

Sounds more like the Skull Of Windows 7.

• Jane MacLaren Walsh, "Legend of the Crystal Skulls," Archaeology, May/June 2008, www.archaeology.org.

 F A C T: According to legend, a Dutch sea captain who wrecked near the Cape of Good Hope in the seventeenth century was punished for blasphemy and tempting fate by having to relive his ordeal for all eternity. The phantom of his ship, the *Flying Dutchman*, is said to haunt the waters off the Cape of Good Hope, bringing doom to any mariner who sees it.

Cape of Good Hope-I Don't-See-That-Thing.

• Angus Konstam, Ghost Ships: Tales of Abandoned, Doomed, and Haunted Vessels (Globe Pequot, 2005), 62.

F A C T: In December 1862, the merchant ship *Mary Celeste* was discovered adrift in the Atlantic Ocean, unmanned and abandoned despite fair-weather. The crew was never found, nor was there any clue as to how or why they vanished.

There can't possibly be any reasonable explanation; no, it could only be aliens or magic holes in the sea or the Chupacabra. Maybe even Tutankhamen's curse.

• Angus Konstam, Ghost Ships: Tales of Abandoned, Doomed, and Haunted Vessels (Globe Pequot, 2005), 78.

F A C T: Some scientists believe that wormholes have the greatest potential for time travel; they could, in theory, permit travel light-years away from Earth in just a fraction of the time required for space travel.

I wish this were true. I'd travel ahead in time and see what joke I came up with for this entry.

• Kevin Bonsor, "How Time Travel Will Work," HowStuffWorks.com, www.science.howstuffworks.com.

F A C T: In 1587, 120 English men and women settled on Roanoke Island off the coast of Virginia, but when the colony's governor travelled back to England for more financial and material resources and returned three years later, the entire colony had vanished.

That fast? I think a glacier could disappear in three years.

• "Top Ten Famous Disappearances," Time.com, www.time.com.

F A C T: In 1918, the U.S. Navy collier *Cyclops* vanished in the Bermuda Triangle shortly after departing Barbados for the United States. Neither the ship nor her crew of 309 sailors was ever seen again. In an official statement, the U.S. government called the Cyclops disappearance 'one of the most baffling mysteries in the annals of the Navy,' as there were no reported German submarines in the area at that time.

No reported submarines. Isn't that sort of the idea of submarines?

• "Seven Disappearances In the Bermuda Triangle," HowStuffWorks.com, www.science. howstuffworks.com.

F A C T: From their home on the island of Crete, the Minoans once dominated the commerce and culture of the eastern Mediterranean. But in 1500BC, their advanced civilization came to a catastrophic end: temples and palaces fell into ruin, viaducts crumbled, and residents died or mysteriously disappeared.

Maybe the Flying Dutchman was holidaying in the Mediterranean and they saw him.

• Frank Joseph, The Destruction of Atlantis: Compelling Evidence of the Sudden Fall of the Legendary Civilization (Inner Traditions/Bear & Company, 2004).

 F A C T: In the mid-nineteenth century, hunters in the Ochamchir region of Abkhazan captured a feral hair-covered woman with ape-like features who is believed to be a survivor of the Neanderthal race. The woman, named Zana by scientists who studied her, was tamed, shaved, and taught how to speak before moving to America and becoming a celebrity.

Now she goes by a different name: Kim Kardashian.

• Colin Wilson and Damon Wilson, The Mammoth Encyclopedia of the Unsolved (Carroll & Graf, 2000).

 F A C T: Ten-year old Benedetto Supino made headlines in the 1980s for his apparent ability to set objects on fire just by looking at them.

This became a problem when a teenaged Ben started checking out girls' arses.

• Worlds Most Incredible Stories (Barnes & Noble Publishing).

 F A C T: Dinosaurs evolved slowly on Earth over millions of years, surviving two distinct periods of mass extinction before dying out completely. The cause of their final, ultimate extinction is still unknown.

I think that I've got it figured out. The Roanoke Island colonists, tired of waiting for their governor, hitched a ride on the Mary Celeste, then dinosaurs ate both the colonists and the crew of the Mary Celeste and stole their boat so that they could sail to Crete and eat the Minoans, too. Then on their way back, the dinosaurs were hijacked by the Jersey Devil and the

Chupacabra, who made them sail the ship around the Cape of Good Hope,
where they all saw the Flying Dutchman and vanished forever.

• "Mass Extinctions and The Evolution Of Dinosaurs," Science Daily, September 30, 2008,
www.sciencedaily.com.
• Bonnie Sachatello-Sawyer and Don and Liza Charlesworth, "Why Did All Dinosaurs Become
Extinct?" in Dinosaurs: The Very Latest Information and Hands-On Activities From the Museum of
the Rockies, Liza Charlesworth and Bonnie Sachatello-Sawyer (Scholastic Professional, 1996).

 F A C T: In 1951, a widow in St Petersburg, Florida was found dead in a chair encircled by soot. Her head was burned to the size of a teacup. Every other part of her body was charred to ash, save her backbone and a portion of her left foot.

Spontaneous combustion is one of the most burning mysteries of our time,
an incendiary topic which often leads to heated debates and flying sparks
on both sides of the issue. Thank you. I'm here all week.

• "Spontaneous Human Combustion," HowStuffWorks.com, www.science.howstuffworks.com.

 F A C T: In 1976, only 16 per cent of Americans said that they believed in ghosts. By 2000, that number had risen to 33 per cent.

In related news, idiots are breeding faster than no idiots.

• Peter Strupp and Alan Dingman, Fat, Dumb, and Ugly: The Decline of the Average American
(Simon & Schuster, 2004).

 F A C T: Seven per cent of Americans believe that Elvis Presley is still alive, even though the singer died in 1977. Interestingly, the percentage is even higher (11 per cent) among people under the age of thirty, the group least likely to be Elvis fans.

Elvis is dead, trust me. If he were alive, he would deny the story that he
died on the crapper. That's just embarrassing.

• "The King's Popularity Contest," CBS News Polls, August 11, 2002, www.cbsnews.com.

GOODBYE CRUEL WORLD!

Bad News about Our World and Why We're All Heading for the Way of the Dodo

FACT: Many of the gases that make up Earth's atmosphere are slowly leaking into space. Hot gases evaporate away, chemical reactions and particle collisions eject atoms and molecules, and asteroids and comets blast out chunks of atmosphere.

My dogs slowly leak gas, too. You don't hear anything, but you know it's there, trust me.

• Kevin J. Zahnle, David C.Catling, and Alfred T. Kamajian, "Our Planet's Leaky Atmosphere," Scientific American, May 2009, www.scientificamerican.com.

FACT: The moon is moving away from Earth at a rate of 3.8cm per year.

We have a man up there measuring it. You should see his ruler.

• Neil F. Comins, Discovering the Essential Universe, 4th ed. (Macmillan, 2008).

FACT: Every year approximately 500 meteorites strike the Earth.

The trick is knowing where.

• John S. Lewis, Physics and Chemistry of the Solar System, 2nd ed. (Academic Press, 2004).

F A C T: The Andromeda galaxy is on a collision course with our galaxy, speeding at 720,000 miles per hour. When the two likely collide in 3 billion years, the results will be catastrophic.

That gives you just enough time to get your driver's license renewed, so go to the DVLA now.

• Peter Douglas Ward and Donald Brownlee, The Life and Death of Planet Earth: How the New Science of Astrobiology Charts the Ultimate Fate of Our World (Macmillan, 2003).

 F A C T: In the future, the depletion of hydrogen will dry out our seas and all but shut down geologic cycles that stabilise our planet's climate. Life might continue, but only in the polar regions.

The polar bears are ready. Eating seals gets boring after a while.

• Kevin J. Zahnle, David C. Catling, and Alfred T. Kamajian, "Our Planet's Leaky Atmosphere," Scientific American, May 2009, www.scientificamerican.com.

 F A C T: Every year, more than 28 million gallons of oil from human activities pour into our rivers, lakes, and streams, an amount more than twice the size of the Exxon Valdez oil spill.

Human activities = oil changes and frying chips.

• "Why Are Our Oceans in Trouble?" Environmental Defense Fund, August 19, 2005, www.edf.org.

 F A C T: About 7.6 billion years from now, the sun will reach its maximum size, extending 20 per cent beyond Earth's orbit and shining 3,000 times brighter than it does today. In its final stage, the sun will collapse into a white dwarf and engulf the Earth.

Mark your calendars!

• Peter Douglas Ward and Donald Brownlee, The Life and Death of Planet Earth: How the New Science of Astrobiology Charts the Ultimate Fate of Our World (Macmillan, 2003).
• David Appell, "The Sun Will Eventually Engulf Earth – Maybe," Scientific American, September 2008, www.scientificamerican.com.

 F A C T: 80 per cent of the waste that humans produce ends up in our oceans, including everything from solid rubbish and sewage to fertilizers, oil, and toxic chemicals.

This is why I never feel guilty about pissing in the sea.

• "Problems: Ocean pollution," World Wildlife Federation, February 29, 2008, www.panda.org.

 FACT: Raw, untreated sewage flows into the sea in many areas of the world, including 80 per cent of urban sewage that ends up in the Mediterranean.

If you're reading this on the toilet, congrats, you just made a nice float for some poor bastard in Crete.

• "Problems: Ocean pollution," World Wildlife Federation, February 29, 2008, www.panda.org.

 FACT: Acid rain is caused by both natural sources like volcanoes and decaying vegetation, and artificial sources like emissions from fossil fuel combustion. It threatens both animal and plant life through acidification of lakes and streams and damage to forests and forest soils.

The brown acid rain is particularly bad, so avoid it. It's giving a lot of people bad trips.

• "Effects of Acid Rain," U.S. Environmental Protection Agency, www.epa.gov.

 FACT: About half of the carbon dioxide emitted by humans in the last 200 years has been absorbed by the Earth's seas, causing fish migration routes to alter, sea levels to rise, coastal erosion to intensify, and currents that move nutrients upward from the deep sea to become disturbed.

If there were oceans on other planets, we could send it there, but we haven't found any yet.

• Dan Shapley, "Natural Resources Being Depleted at Record Rates," The Daily Green, September 13, 2007, www.thedailygreen.com.

 FACT: In Alaska, more than 200 communities are threatened by rising sea levels that cause tides to extend about three meters further inland each year.

Alaska has 200 communities?

• Larry West, "Scholars Predict 50 Million Environmental Refugees by 2010," About.com, www.environment.about.com.

F A C T: The state of Louisiana loses about sixty-five square kilometers of productive land every year to erosion by the sea.

Louisiana has productive land?

• Larry West, "Scholars Predict 50 Million Environmental Refugees by 2010," About.com, www.environment.about.com.

 F A C T: Experts say that more than 1,000 square kilometers of productive land is lost annually in Morocco, Tunisia, and Libya to desertification.

Morocco, Tunisia, and Libya have productive land?

• Larry West, "Scholars Predict 50 Million Environmental Refugees by 2010," About.com, www.environment.about.com.

 F A C T: China's Gobi desert is expanding at the rate of over 10,000 square kilometers per year, overtaking productive soil and threatening the livelihood of many villages.

The ants are loving it, though.

• Larry West, "Scholars Predict 50 Million Environmental Refugees by 2010," About.com, www.environment.about.com.

 F A C T: Category 4 and 5 hurricanes have doubled in the last 30 years.

In case you haven't watched the news. Ever.

• K. Emanuel, "Increasing destructiveness of tropical cyclones over the past 30 years," Nature, August 4, 2005, 686–688, "What is Global Warming?" An Inconvenient Truth, www.climatecrisis.net.

 F A C T: Just a slight increase in sea levels could submerge most of the Maldives. President Mohamed Nasheed has proposed to relocate the entire 300,000 person nation to India, Sri Lanka, or Australia.

If Sri Lanka is safer than where you live, you need to move anyway.

• Larry West, "Scholars Predict 50 Million Environmental Refugees by 2010," About.com, www.environment.about.com.
• Nicholas Schmidle, "Wanted: A New Home for My Country," New York Times, May 8, 2009, www.nytimes.com.

F A C T: New Zealand has agreed to accept the almost 12,000 citizens of the Pacific island state of Tuvalu if rising sea levels make the island uninhabitable.

New Zealanders don't want to die alone when rising sea levels make their islands uninhabitable, too.

• Larry West, "Scholars Predict 50 Million Environmental Refugees by 2010," About.com, www.environment.about.com.

 F A C T: Deaths caused by global warming will double in the next twenty-five years to 300,000 people annually.

Dying people often complain of being cold; I wonder if that happens when you die of global warming.

• World Health Organization, "What is Global Warming?" An Inconvenient Truth, www.climatecrisis.net.

 F A C T: Libya recorded the Earth's highest temperature in 1922: 136°F (58°C).

But it was a dry heat.

• "Fun Science Facts You Didn't Know," High Tech Science, www.hightechscience.org.

 F A C T: Thanks to global warming, the Arctic Ocean could be free of ice in summer by 2050.

What if your name was 'Global Warming'? That would be awful. You'd get blamed for everything.

• W. Krabill and others, "Greenland Ice Sheet: Increased coastal thinning," Geophysical Research Letters, December 28, 2004, "What is Global Warming?" An Inconvenient Truth, www.climatecrisis.net.
• Impact of a Warming Arctic: Arctic Climate Impact Assessment (Cambridge, UK: Cambridge University Press, 2004), "What is Global Warming?" An Inconvenient Truth, www.climatecrisis.net.

 F A C T: The 2008 Great Sichuan Earthquake in China was felt as far away as Shanghai, over 1,000 miles from the quake's epicentre. Nearly 70,000 people died, and more than 118,000 were seriously injured. Thousands of Chinese are still missing and presumed dead.

You think?!

• "Eight of the Most Devastating Deadly Land Disasters," WebEcoist, www.webecoist.com.

F A C T: More than 2,000 people died in 1960 when a tsunami hit the coast of Chile with a massive thirty-foot wave, flooding 500 coastal miles and triggering the largest earthquake in the twentieth century.

The real tragedy is that all those people missed the '60s, which were a blast.

• "Six Chilling Ice Storms, Tsunamis and Floods," WebEcoist, www.webecoist.com.

 F A C T: In 1902, a landslide of boiling mud spilled into the sea on the island of Martinique, causing a tsunami that killed hundreds. Three days later, Mount Pelee exploded, oblitreating the town of St Pierre with an avalanche of hot lava. Of 30,000 residents, only two survived.

The boiling mud would've been enough to send me packing. Why was anyone around three days later for the volcano eruption?

• "Eight of the Most Devastating Deadly Land Disasters," WebEcoist. www.webecoist.com.
• David Wallechinsky, The New Book of Lists: The Original Compendium of Curious Information [Canon gate U.S., 2005], 397.

F A C T: When Colombia's volcanic mountain Nevado del Ruiz exploded in 1984, the resulting mudslide buried the nearby town of Armero, killing more than 23,000 people.

No one heard it coming?

• "Eight of the Most Devastating Deadly Land Disasters," WebEcoist. www.webecoist.com.

 F A C T: The world's seas contain enough salt to cover every continent to a depth of almost 500 feet.

Which is the same amount needed to make lentils edible.

• "Fifty Weird Science Tidbits & Oddities," Science News Review, February 11, 2009, www.sciencenewsreview.com.

 F A C T: The 1991 eruption of Mount Pinatubo on the Philippine island of Luzon caused a sulfuric haze around the world, a global drop in temperatures, and a spike in ozone damage. Most residents were evacuated before billions of tons of ash, magma, and debris destroyed it.

The worldwide drop in temperature was quickly corrected by global warming, though, so no worries there.

• Matt Rosenberg, "Mount Pinatubo Eruption," About.com, August 5, 2007, www.geography.about.com.

 F A C T: Four years of deforestation shares the same carbon footprint as every air flight from the dawn of aviation through to 2025.

Deforestation doesn't give you free soft drinks, though.

• Debra Ronca, "How Deforestation Works," HowStuffWorks.com, www.science.howstuffworks.com

 F A C T: Depletion of the Earth's ozone layer aggravates health effects caused by exposure to UV radiation. Even a 10 per cent loss of ozone could cause an additional 300,000 skin cancers and up to 1.75 million more cases of cataracts worldwide every year.

It's easier to get a tan now, though.

• "Ultraviolet Radiation and Health," World Health Organizations, www.who.int.

 F A C T: Burping cows emit up to 100 gallons of methane gas per animal each day, joining other livestock to create nearly a third of man-made methane emissions annually. Methane is a greenhouse gas that warms Earth's atmosphere at twenty-one times the rate of carbon dioxide.

You don't even want to know about their farts.

• Bettina Gartner, "How Better-Fed Cows Could Cool the Planet," Christian Science Monitor, August 16, 2007, www.csmonitor.com.

 F A C T: Burning rainforests account for roughly 30 per cent of the carbon dioxide released in the air.

We shouldn't burn the rainforests. We need to save them to burn when we run out of oil and need the heat.

• Tom Harris, "How Rainforests Work," HowStuffWorks.com, www.science.howstuffworks.com.

FACT: Biologists believe that the flora and fauna of rainforests holds the cure to many diseases. Rainforests cover 7 per cent of the Earth but are inhabited by 50 per cent of the plant and animal species of the world – species becoming extinct as deforestation shrinks rainforest areas.

Deforestation is named after DeForest Kelley, famed tree-cutter and actor who played Dr Leonard 'Bones' McCoy on Star Trek.

• Debra Ronca, "How Deforestation Works," HowStuffWorks.com, www.science.howstuffworks.com.

 FACT: One gallon of used motor oil can ruin approximately 1 million gallons of fresh water.

That's why we seal up the barrels before we throw them in to the sea.

• "Why We Should Recycle Used Oil," L.A. County Department Of Public Works, www.dpw.lacounty.gov.

 FACT: In 1979 Skylab, the first U.S. space station, crashed to Earth in pieces.

So did David Bowie, but nobody cared about that, either.

• "Fun Science Facts You Didn't Know," High Tech Science, www.hightechscience.org

 FACT: Because of time zones, if you fly from London to New York by Concorde, you can arrive two hours before you departed.

I knew the Concorde was fast, but Jesus!

• "Fun Science Facts You Didn't Know," High Tech Science, www.hightechscience.org.

 FACT: New research predicts that the Earth's temperature could rise by 3°–6°C (37.4°–42.8°F) by the close of the twenty-first century, enough to have a serious impact on human life through rising sea levels, flooding, widespread drought, anymore.

I plan to be long gone by then, so good luck with that, kids.

• Michael D. Lemonick, "Global Warming: Beyond the Tipping Point," Scientific American, October 2008, www.sciam.com.

F A C T: Ebola is a lethal virus in humans and has no cure. The source of the disease is unclear, but outbreaks usually occur after droughts and downpours in central Africa, which will only increase as the planet warms.

After droughts and downpours? So, it occurs whenever it's raining or not raining. At least it doesn't occur all the time.

• David Biello, "Deadly by the Dozen: 12 Diseases Climate Change May Worsen," Scientific American, October 8, 2008, www.sciam.com.

F A C T: Cholera bacteria thrives in warm waters and causes diarrhoea so severe that it can kill someone within a week. With no improved sanitation, the rise in global temperatures will lead to deadly outbreaks.

After crapping your brains out for a week, death is probably a relief.

• David Biello, "Deadly by the Dozen: 12 Diseases Climate Change May Worsen," Scientific American, October 8, 2008, www.sciam.com.

F A C T: Droughts caused by global warming are likely to bring livestock and wildlife into closer proximity as they compete for water, thus increasing the risk of TB among both humans and animals.

And the number of livestock is likely to decrease.

• David Biello, "Deadly by the Dozen: 12 Diseases Climate Change May Worsen," Scientific American, October 8, 2008, www.sciam.com.

F A C T: A malaria-like disease called babesiosis, which is carried by ticks and is native to tropical climates, is spreading to cooler climes and has recently appeared in places like Italy and Long Island, New York. Babesiosis is rare in humans but that could change with increased global warming.

Babesiosis sounds like something that would turn a plain woman into a fittie, but I don't really think malaria has that ability.

• David Biello, "Deadly by the Dozen: 12 Diseases Climate Change May Worsen," Scientific American, October 8, 2008, www.sciam.com.

F A C T: One in four mammals is now threatened with extinction from deforestation, hunting, and climate change.

*Do we get to pick which ones? Because armadillos seem pretty pointless,
but we're going to need the cows.*

• "View: The Truth about Trash," Scientific American, January 9, 2009, www.sciam.com.

 F A C T: Hurricane Ike lasted thirteen days, took 114 lives, and
caused $10 billion in damage as it rolled through Cuba, Haiti.

That's a lot more damage than Ike Turner ever did.

• "Terrifying Tornadoes, Wind Storms and Hurricanes," Web-Ecoist, October 22, 2008,
www.webecoist.com.

 F A C T: In 2004, tens of thousands of people were displaced,
injured, and made homeless when Hurricane Katrina hit the Gulf
Coast. A combination of 175-mph winds, massive storm surge, lack of
preparedness, and inadequate government response turned Katrina,
one of the most powerful hurricanes in America's history, into an epic
disaster.

In case you happened to miss it on the news. For a year.

• "Terrifying Tornadoes, Wind Storms and Hurricanes," Web-Ecoist, October 22, 2008,
www.webecoist.com.

 F A C T: Hurricane Katrina decimated New Orleans, but also affected
90,000 square miles of Louisiana, Mississippi, and Alabama, claiming
more than 1,300 lives across the region. Dead bodies were still being
found eight months after the hurricane.

*It must be delightful to find a corpse after eight months. I might have to
add that to my bucket list.*

• "Terrifying Tornadoes, Wind Storms and Hurricanes," Web-Ecoist, October 22, 2008,
www.webecoist.com.

 F A C T: Tornadoes are the products of thunderstorms that pop
up suddenly and without warning. They produce winds that can exceed
250 mph and can damage areas more than a mile wide and fifty
miles long.

For once I will resist the urge to make a fart joke here. Why? Because you're probably expecting it, and I hate being predictable.

• "Terrifying Tornadoes, Wind Storms and Hurricanes," Web-Ecoist, October 22, 2008, www.webecoist.com.

 FACT: Lightning strikes the Earth more than 5,000 times every minute.

The trick is knowing where.

• Kevin T. Pickering and Lewis A. Owen, An Introduction to Global Environmental Issues, 2nd ed. (Routledge, 1997).

 FACT: About 10 per cent of lightning-strike victims are killed. Of those who survive, 70 per cent suffer serious long-term effects from injuries that include severe burns and can also lead to personality change, permanent brain damage, and memory loss.

I'm thinking that death might be the way to go when it comes to lightning.

• "Flash Facts About Lightning," National Geographic News, June 24, 2005, www.news.nationalgeographic.com.

 FACT: Take shelter when your hair stands on end in a storm: it often means that positive charges are rising through you, reaching up towards the negatively charged part of the storm and making you a target for lightning.

Or it just means that you're Jedward.

• "Flash Facts About Lightning," National Geographic News, June 24, 2005, www.news.nationalgeographic.com.

 FACT: Once lightning enters a structure, it may run through the electrical system, phone lines, plumbing, even TV and radio antennas and cables. It is also possible for lightning to pass through metal in concrete walls or flooring.

Persistent little bastard isn't it?

• "Flash Facts About Lightning," National Geographic News, June 24, 2005, www.news.nationalgeographic.com.

F A C T: Floods are one of the most severe weather events and a leading cause of weather-related deaths. Just six inches of fast-moving water is enough to knock an adult off his feet.

Unless that adult is Kirstie Alley or one of those contestants on The Biggest Loser – they require a little more.

• Rachelle Oblack, "How to Stay Safe in a Flood," About.com, www.weather.about.com.

 F A C T: The deadliest type of flood is a flashflood, caused when heavy rain leads to sudden surges of water. These waters can destroy buildings and make roads impassable, preventing escape and assistance.

This is why everyone should own a surfboard.

• Rachelle Oblack, "How to Stay Safe in a Flood," About.com, www.weather.about.com.

 F A C T: In 2007, flooding on the banks of the Huai River displaced 2 billion rats in central China, which destroyed over 6,000 square miles of cropland and caused an estimated $3.13 billion in damage.

Most of them relocated to London and are doing just fine.

• "Chinese Floods Displace Billions of Rats, Mice; Raise Fears of Disease." USA Today, On Deadline, July 12, 2007, http://blogs.usatoday.com.

 F A C T: A 1998 storm pelted Quebec, Canada with freezing rain and enveloped the city in a layer of cement-like ice, causing thirty deaths and weeks of power cuts for millions of Canadians.

When did Canada get electricity?

• "Six Chilling Ice Storms, Tsunamis and Floods," WebEcoist, www.webecoist.com.

 F A C T: For the last fifteen years, Indonesia has been plagued by so many wildfires that breathing air near the burn sites is at times equivalent to smoking eighty packs of cigarettes a day.

But for Indonesians on a budget, it's a lot cheaper.

• "Six Worst Raging Fires and Explosive Volcanoes," WebEcoist, www.webecoist.com.

F A C T: The most destructive volcanic eruption of the twentieth century occurred in 1991 at Mount Pinatubo in the Philippines. The blast was so powerful that it caused a global sulfuric haze and a temperature drop of almost one degree Fahrenheit around the world.

But don't worry, global warming took care of that temperature drop within a day or two.

• "Six Worst Raging Fires and Explosive Volcanoes," Web-Ecoist, www.webecoist.com.

F A C T: Scientists have discovered evidence of an asteroid collision 3½ billion years ago that was the likely cause of a massive tsunami which swept around the Earth several times, flooding everything except the highest mountains and wiping out nearly all life on land.

So by the time you get your cave dried out and recarve all those stick figures on the wall, here comes the fucker again.

• "Tsunami Facts: How They Form, Warning Signs, and Safety Tips," National Geographic News, April 2, 2007, www.news.nationalgeographic.com.

F A C T: Tsunami waves can be as long as sixty miles, occur as far apart as an hour, and be powerful enough to traverse entire oceans without losing significant energy. The Indian Ocean tsunami in 2004 travelled as far as 3,000 miles to Africa and still arrived with enough force to kill people and destroy property.

Who sticks around for an hour after the first tsunami hits?

• "Tsunami Facts: How They Form, Warning Signs, and Safety Tips," National Geographic News, April 2, 2007, www.news.nationalgeographic.com.

F A C T: Tsunamis can travel unnoticed in deep water as fast as 500 miles an hour, and cross an entire ocean in less than a day.

Sneaky bastards.

• "Tsunami Facts: How They Form, Warning Signs, and Safety Tips," National Geographic News, April 2, 2007, www.news.nationalgeographic.com.